YALE FOOTBALL

A selection of football memorabilia rests on the Yale fence. The fence was originally located on the New Haven Green, where students often played football in the 1800s. Captains of all Yale sports now have their captain's photograph taken on a section of the fence located in the Yale Athletic Department offices. (Photograph by Michael Marsland.)

On the front cover: Walter Camp is pictured in Yale's 1879 team photograph. (Courtesy of Yale Athletic Department archives.)

On the back cover: The Yale Bowl hosts more than 50,000 people for the Yale-Harvard game. (Photograph by Bill O'Brien; courtesy of Yale Sports Publicity Department.)

Cover background: Carm Cozza can be seen on the sideline. (Photograph by Sabby Frinzi.)

YALE FOOTBALL

Sam Rubin

ARCADIA
PUBLISHING

Published by Arcadia Publishing
Charleston, South Carolina

Library of Congress Catalog Card Number: 2006923707

For all general information contact Arcadia Publishing at:
Telephone 843-853-2070
Fax 843-853-0044
E-mail sales@arcadiapublishing.com
For customer service and orders:
Toll-Free 1-888-313-2665

Visit us on the Internet at www.arcadiapublishing.com

In memory of Dick Galiette.

CONTENTS

ACKNOWLEDGMENTS

Unless otherwise noted, all images are courtesy of the Yale Athletic Department archives. Whenever possible, the photographers have been credited.

Special thanks go to Bob Barton, Carm Cozza, Sabby Frinzi, Dick Galiette, Ron Vaccaro, the New Haven Register, the Yale Athletic Department, the Yale Football Association, the Yale Sports Publicity Department, and the Yale University Library.

Thanks also to the many authors who have previously documented Yale football history, particularly Tim Cohane (*The Yale Football Story*) and Thomas Bergin (*The Game, Gridiron Glory*).

INTRODUCTION

When 20 Yale men gathered at New Haven's Hamilton Park on November 16, 1872, for a game of football against Columbia, the sport was in its infancy. Many feared Yale's first game would be its last.

Over 130 years later, with the Elis still going strong, the significance of that day is apparent. The support for that first game merited three more the next year, then another three the following year. In 1875, Yale's schedule expanded to four games, including its first against Harvard. In 1876, Walter Camp arrived on the Yale campus, putting the pieces in place for the formation of the game as we know it.

Camp joined the intercollegiate football rules committee, and in 1880 introduced the concept of plays from scrimmage and other innovations. Numerical values for touchdowns and other scoring plays were soon developed.

From 1879 through 1884, Yale went 36-0-5, regularly winning national championships. Yale's 1888 squad outscored its opponents 698-0, and at the turn of the century the renowned 1900 team went 12-0.

All was not right in the growing game, however, as brutal "wedge" formations came to dominate play. The sport reached a turning point in 1905, when Pres. Theodore Roosevelt commanded Camp and other rulemakers to reduce the violence. That led to the formation of the National Collegiate Athletic Association and the legalization of the forward pass.

The Bulldog machine pressed on, recording a 10-0 season in 1909. That campaign culminated with a win over Harvard in what was billed as the "Battle of the Giants." It soon became apparent that Yale Field, the team's home since 1884, was not suited for the large crowds the Elis were attracting. The opening of the Yale Bowl in 1914 ushered in a new era.

World War I brought college football to a halt, but after the war fans once again jammed onto trolleys to make their way out to the Yale Bowl. They streamed in even during the Depression, as local boy Albie Booth's exploits captured imaginations. Yale's upset win at Princeton in 1934 made the Elis' 11 "Iron Men" famous—they were the last to play an entire game without substitution. One of those men, Larry Kelley, would win the Heisman Trophy in 1936. A year later, Clint Frank earned the same honor.

After World War II, the presence of war veterans on team rosters changed the landscape of college football. One of those GIs, Levi Jackson, became Yale's first African American captain in 1949. The end of the war also saw the first steps toward the formation of the Ivy League. When the league began playing a full schedule in 1956, Yale fittingly claimed the first championship. Four years later the Bulldogs won again and posted a perfect (9-0) overall record.

The 1960s were a turbulent time in America, but for Yale football the decade was marked by the start of an era of stability. Carm Cozza took over as head coach in 1965 for a 32-year run, and the Bulldogs won three straight Ivy League titles starting in 1967. Yale celebrated its football centennial in 1972, and by 1974 the Bulldogs were back on top of the Ivy League. That started a run of six titles in an eight-year span. Cozza's retirement in 1996 began a new era, and Yale brought home its 13th Ivy League championship in 1999.

Yale recently began work on the restoration of the Yale Bowl, ensuring that it will remain a suitably grand place for future generations of Bulldogs—just a few blocks from the site of that 1872 meeting with Columbia.

The Yale Precision Marching Band has been a part of the atmosphere at games for decades.

1

WALTER CAMP AND

YALE'S NEW SPORT

Entering its first football game against Columbia on November 16, 1872, Yale was anxious about the viability of the sport. "Probably it was thought that if the game were to fail in attracting spectators, the failure would be an indication that football was not to be continued as a sport in Yale College," captain David Schaff said. The game featured 20 players per side on a field that was 400 feet by 250 feet. (Courtesy of Manuscripts and Archives, Yale University Library.)

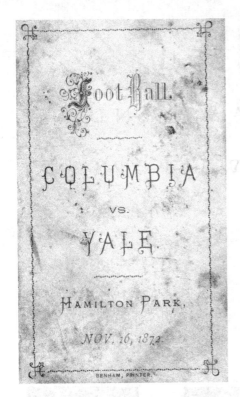

Despite raw and chilly conditions, 400 spectators showed up for Yale's first football game, which resembled soccer more than anything else. Yale's Tommy Sherman kicked the first goal and Lew Irwin kicked two more for the 3-0 win over Columbia. The interest the game generated led captain David Schaff to note that "one of the purposes of the game had been secured. Football was given a place of respectability among undergraduate interests."

David Schaff had attended the Rugby School in England and played football there prior to entering Yale in 1870. He led the call for a meeting of students on October 31, 1872, that resulted in the formation of the Yale Football Association, the first formal body for governing the sport at Yale. Schaff was elected president of the association and captain of the team, and arranged for Yale's inaugural game. Ironically, he was injured in practice the day before the contest and was unable to play.

Yale's 1873 team, which went 3-0, was the first to play with just 11 men per side, doing so against the Eton players. Team size varied—11, 15, or 20—for the first eight years that Yale played.

In 1873, Yale, Columbia, Rutgers, and Princeton drew up the first intercollegiate football rules in America, codifying a soccer-style game in which the use of one's hands to carry the ball was prohibited. Harvard declined an invitation to participate because it preferred the "Boston" rules, which allowed the use of hands. Yale and Harvard thus did not play each other until 1875. After battling in baseball (starting in 1868) and crew (starting in 1852), the two rivals finally met in football after agreeing to "concessionary" rules that allowed the use of hands to carry the ball as Harvard preferred. The Cantabs won 4-0, but the Bulldogs soon mastered the new rules. Yale won the next meeting 1-0.

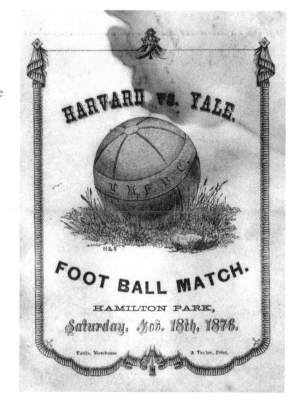

The site of Yale's first game, and first game against Harvard, was Hamilton Park. The park was located in the shadow of West Rock in the area bounded by Whalley Avenue, Pendleton Street, and the West River—less than a mile from where Yale currently plays. (Courtesy of the New Haven Colony Historical Society.)

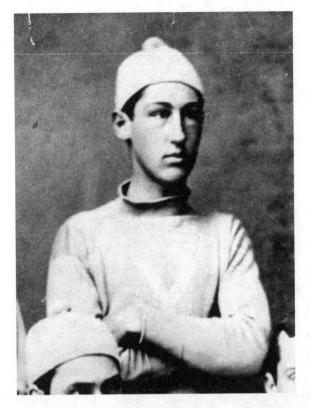

When halfback Walter Camp arrived at Yale in 1876, football was in its formative stages. Having played rugby in prep school, Camp joined the football team at Yale and served as captain in 1878 and 1879. He was elected captain again in 1881 but had to stop playing due to his medical school studies. A knee injury in practice ended his playing days after the third game of the 1882 season.

WALTER CAMP AND YALE'S NEW SPORT

Before becoming a renowned painter and illustrator, Frederic Remington was a Yale art school student who earned two letters with the football team. He reportedly showed up for the 1880 Yale-Harvard game having dipped his jersey in blood from a slaughterhouse to appear more "business-like." After leaving Yale he made his way west to clerk in a general store and serve as a stockman on a ranch. Upon his return to the East he set about recording his vision of the vanishing American West, with his work appearing in magazines such as Harper's Weekly and Collier's. Remington immortalized the 1890 Yale-Princeton game in *Foot-Ball—A Collision at the Ropes* for Harper's. That game was a 32-0 Eli victory that gave Yale the Intercollegiate Football Association championship with a 13-1 record. (Courtesy of Yale University Art Gallery, Whitney Collection of Sporting Art, given in memory of Harry Payne Whitney [1894] and Payne Whitney [1898] by Francis P. Garvan [1897], June 2, 1932.)

Football in Walter Camp's early years was very different from the game of today. He joined the rules committee in 1878 and went on to attend every convention until his death in 1925. Prior to 1880, even as a team advanced the ball it risked losing it with each rugby-style scrum. Camp recognized this as a haphazard way of determining possession. At the 1880 convention, he convinced his fellow delegates to replace the "scrummage" with the "scrimmage": the team with the ball would put it in play by having a player snap it back to a teammate—the quarter-back—using his foot (by 1890, players were allowed to use their hands instead of their feet). The 1880 convention also saw the change to 11 men per side instead of 15, thanks to Camp. Two years later he introduced the concept of downs (originally three downs to either advance five yards or lose 10 yards) to keep offenses from monopolizing the ball. A year after that came numerical scoring: five points for a field goal, four for a goal after a touchdown, two for a touchdown, and one for a safety. (Courtesy of Manuscripts and Archives, Yale University Library.)

Guard Ray Tompkins captained Yale to national championships in 1882 and 1883. He passed away in 1918. His widow, Sarah Wey Tompkins, passed away in 1929. In 1931, it was announced that she had left $3 million to Yale for two buildings, Payne Whitney Gymnasium and Ray Tompkins House. Ray Tompkins House, once the football dormitory, is home to the Yale Athletic Department offices.

Quarterback Henry "Deac" Twombly helped the Elis to a 21-0-1 record from 1881 to 1883. That included a 2-0 win over Michigan in 1881 in which Twombly excelled on defense (the concept of separate "platoons" for offense, defense, and special teams was still years away). "Watching their quarterback, I soon got onto his signals, and got started at the same time as the ball," he said. The next year Yale began using voice signals, including "look out quick Deac" to indicate that Twombly would run over guard.

After 12 seasons at privately owned Hamilton Park, the Yale Football Association wanted a field of its own. Two members of the class of 1881—Adrian S. Van de Graaff and Henry S. White—spearheaded the purchase of land on the south side of Derby Avenue two miles west of the campus. Yale Field hosted its first football game on October 1, 1884—a 31-0 win over Wesleyan.

When halfback Wyllys Terry got the ball behind his own goal line against Wesleyan on November 5, 1884, everyone thought he would take a safety, which would enable Yale to put the ball back in play from its 25-yard line. Terry had other ideas, taking off and dodging would-be tacklers. At midfield—the 55-yard line—he evaded his last pursuer, racing ahead for Yale's second score of the game, which Yale won 46-0. The 110-yard run was the longest in Yale history. The field was shortened to 100 yards in 1912.

WALTER CAMP AND YALE'S NEW SPORT

Prior to 1888, Yale employed a system of graduate coaching through which alumni returned to New Haven to help out the captains. Walter Camp was one of those graduates, though his duties with the New Haven Clock Company often kept him away. In 1888, Camp married and settled in New Haven, enabling him to develop a more formal system. He oversaw the head field coach, usually the captain from the previous season, who was appointed by the current captain. Camp also received help from his wife, Allie, who attended practice more regularly than he could due to his duties with the clock company. She took notes and shared them with him over dinner. Yale posted a 67-2-0 record under Camp from 1888 to 1892.

A rules change in 1888 that moved the tackling boundary from the waist to the knees made it harder for runners to break loose, and that led to a style of play designed to offset the advantage for the defense. Teams began concentrating on mass and momentum formations, with linemen and backs grouped closely together to hammer away at the point of attack. The "wedge" dominated, and with it the game became more violent.

"Pa Corbin's long face and handlebar mustache gave him a majestic air, and made him look much older than his 24 years," wrote Pudge Heffelfinger. Corbin, whose real first name was William, was Walter Camp's first captain and a center. "The captain should be the real leader," Corbin said. "He should be able to say 'come on' instead of 'go on.' He should be a strategist, always checking the signals and often changing them."

One of Yale's greatest teams, the 1888 squad ran up a 13-0 record, defeating its opponents 698-0. The final game of the season was the only close one, a 10-0 victory over Princeton thanks to two field goals (then worth five points each) from Billy Bull (third row, right). The defensive effort was keyed by Pudge Heffelfinger (third row, third from left), who stymied Princeton's V-wedge attack by taking a running start and jumping at the chest of the lead man. Heffelfinger was one of five College Football Hall of Famers on the squad, a group that also included center Pa Corbin (holding ball), coach Walter Camp, end Amos Alonzo Stagg (second row, far left), and guard George Woodruff (third row, second from left, inducted as a coach). Along with Heffelfinger and Stagg, tackle Charles Gill (third row, fourth from left) gave Yale three representatives on the first All-America team in 1889, which appeared in sportswriter Caspar Whitney's *The Week's Sport* magazine. Camp popularized the All-America team concept, and the foundation named after him selects a "Walter Camp All-America Team" to this day.

Hall of famer William Walter "Pudge" Heffelfinger (left) came to Yale from Minneapolis, where he was credited with organizing his high school's first football team. He was an All-American at guard from 1889 through 1891. Contrary to his nickname, "Pudge" weighed no more than 205 pounds and was a phenomenally conditioned athlete. "Heffelfinger was the fastest big man I ever saw," said Walter Camp. After leaving Yale, Heffelfinger played for the Allegheny Athletic Association in a win over the Pittsburgh Athletic Club on November 12, 1892. He was paid $500 to play, making him the first professional football player. Hall of famer Thomas Lee "Bum" McClung (right) was an All-American at back for Yale in 1890. While records from that era are unofficial, he is believed to have scored at least 510 points, a Yale record. He eventually returned to Yale as treasurer in 1904. Five years later, he was named treasurer of the United States.

Named to the first All-America team in 1889, end Amos Alonzo Stagg went on to earn enshrinement in both the College Football Hall of Fame and the Basketball Hall of Fame (he brought the game to the University of Chicago, where he was a coach). An accomplished pitcher at Yale, he turned down the chance to go professional in baseball. "I never did a wiser thing," he said. "If it is money that the college man wants, he ought to be able to make more on a real job than by peddling a physical skill. If it is fame, let him go after a brand that won't turn green and shiny in the seat before he is 30."

Hall of famer George Woodruff was a principal before coming to Yale in 1885. Having never played football, he nevertheless made the university's 11 and lettered at guard for four years. When he returned to help coach in 1889 he was credited with introducing the pulling guard, putting Pudge Heffelfinger in that role. Woodruff studied law at the University of Pennsylvania and coached Penn's football team, registering a 124-15-2 record. Later he became an assistant attorney general and acting secretary of the interior under Pres. Theodore Roosevelt.

In 1889, Yale student Andrew B. Graves spotted an animal in a New Haven blacksmith's shop that looked like "a cross between an alligator and a horned toad." Graves bought the dog, gave it a bath, and dubbed his new pet "Handsome Dan." The dog accompanied him everywhere, including football games. Dan's penchant for barking after Yale scores earned him the status of mascot. After Handsome Dan passed away in 1898, it would be 35 years before another Dan walked the Yale campus, but the mascot has been a tradition since.

After graduating in 1891, halfback Henry "Harry" Williams taught at Siglar's Preparatory School at Newburgh-on-Hudson, New York. "While there, by invitation of the officers at West Point, I went to West Point every Saturday and coached the football team," he said. In 1900, he was hired as coach at Minnesota. Williams compiled a 136-33-11 record there, devising the famous "Minnesota Shift" formation. He was enshrined in the College Football Hall of Fame in 1951.

George Sanford, who chalked the lines on Yale Field as a youngster, lettered in 1891 and 1892 and went on to earn recognition as Yale's all-time center in a 1927 poll. Sanford coached at Columbia and Rutgers (with a stop at Yale as an assistant) from 1899 through 1923 and was inducted into the College Football Hall of Fame in 1971.

UNIVERSITY OF NOTRE DAME

Notre Dame, Ind. Sept 20th 1892

Walter Camp:

Dear Sir:

I want to ask a favor of you. Will you kindly furnish me with some points on the best way to develop a good Foot Ball Team. I am an Instructor connected with this University and have been asked to coach the team. I know something of the Rugby game, but would like to find out the best manner to handle the men. I have seen a good many Yale games (as I come from New Haven. You can find out about me from Dr. Seaver.) And knowing you are an authority on the game, I would welcome any points you might give me. Hoping that I am

Walter Camp received the following letter, dated September 20, 1892: "I want to ask a favor of you. Will you kindly furnish me with some points on the best way to develop a good Foot Ball Team. I am an Instructor connected with this University and have been asked to coach the team . . . I have seen a good many Yale games . . . and knowing that you are an authority on the game, I would welcome any points you might give me." The letter was signed by James H. Kivlan of the University of Notre Dame. The two legendary football powers would meet just once on the gridiron—a 28-0 Yale win in 1914. Years later, famed Notre Dame coach Knute Rockne was asked where he got the idea for the Notre Dame shift. "Where everything else in football came from—Yale," he said. (Courtesy of Walter Camp Papers, Manuscripts and Archives, Yale University Library.)

Walter Camp said that end Frank Hinkey "drifted through the interference like a disembodied spirit." While estimates of the five-foot-nine-inch Hinkey's playing weight vary between 135 and 157 pounds, the ferocity of his tackles is unquestioned. He was a key figure in the 1892 Yale-Harvard game, neutralizing Harvard's "flying wedge" and stopping the Cantabs at the Yale seven-yard line to preserve a 6-0 victory. The taciturn Hinkey earned the nickname "Silent" but his teammates respected—and perhaps feared—him. He captained the team in 1893 and 1894 and was a four-time All-American. Named to Walter Camp's All-Time All-America Team in 1910, Hinkey was elected to the College Football Hall of Fame in 1951. "He was the greatest football player of all time," said legendary coach Pop Warner. "He was the personification of two of the greatest attributes of the great football player: determination and fighting spirit."

Fullback Frank Butterworth was a two-time All-American. In the three seasons that he lettered (1892 to 1894), the Bulldogs went 39-1-0. Butterworth scored 11 touchdowns in Yale's 1892 national championship season, and while his production dropped off due to injury in 1893, he did score the lone touchdown in a 6-0 win over Harvard. (Courtesy of Walter Camp Papers, Manuscripts and Archives, Yale University Library.)

A crowd of 50,000 was on hand for Yale's game against Princeton at Manhattan Field in New York in 1893. Games against Harvard at that time drew crowds of 20,000. (Photograph by J. C. Hemment, Pioneer Action Photographer, for Frank Leslie's Weekly.)

Hall of fame guard William Orville
Hickok was as passionate on the field as his
nickname—"Wild Bill"—would indicate.
An All-American in 1893 and 1894, he was
a student of the game and went on to coach
at Carlisle. Hickok was also the national
collegiate shot put and 16-pound hammer
throw champion for three consecutive years.

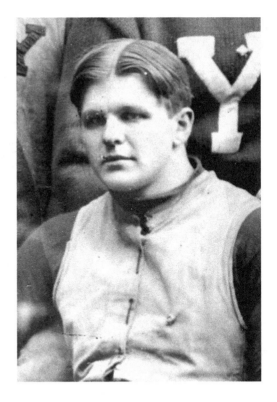

A letter winner from 1893 to 1895, hall of famer Samuel
Brinckerhoff Thorne earned All-America honors at
halfback as a senior. In his final game he scored two
touchdowns, set up a touchdown with a 45-yard punt
return, kicked two conversions, and blocked a punt to lead
Yale to a 20-10 victory over Princeton.

The growing rivalry between Yale and Harvard reached an extreme in 1894. One newspaper labeled it "the roughest Harvard-Yale game in history," noting that "numerous players on both teams were seriously injured and several had to be carried off the field in stretchers." The *World*, shown here, summed up the game with portraits of the injured. After a Harvard player suffered a broken collarbone, Frank Hinkey took the blame and also took a punch to the face from a Harvard player. "My friend," Hinkey said, "if you hit me another blow like that, you will break your hand." The Bulldogs prevailed, 12-4, finishing as national champions with a school-record 16 wins and no defeats. The violence attracted worldwide attention and led to a cessation of the series for two years.

2

GIANTS

Some of Yale's early games took place at the Polo Grounds in New York, including one against Carlisle, a school for Native Americans, in 1897. The Elis claimed a 24-9 victory—and a step towards equality—that day. "There were twenty-two men in perfect condition . . . meeting in equal numbers, man against man, on equal terms," wrote the *New York Times*. (Photograph by Brown Brothers; courtesy of Walter Camp Papers, Manuscripts and Archives, Yale University Library.)

For football fans in the early 1900s, Yale's most recognizable player was a fictional one. Frank Merriwell made his debut in *Street and Smith's Tip Top Weekly* in 1896. Brought to life by Gilbert Patten (writing under the pseudonym Burt L. Standish), Merriwell's stories of heroism sold at a rate of 200,000 copies per week at the height of their popularity. (Courtesy of Manuscripts and Archives, Yale University Library.)

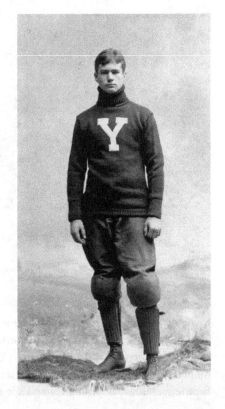

Hall of fame guard Francis Gordon Brown earned All-America honors from 1897 through 1900. He also excelled off the field, where he was a member of Phi Beta Kappa. Brown died of diabetes in 1911 at the age of 31. His classmates established the Francis Gordon Brown Memorial Prize, given to the junior "who most closely approaches the standard of good scholarship and character set by Francis Gordon Brown."

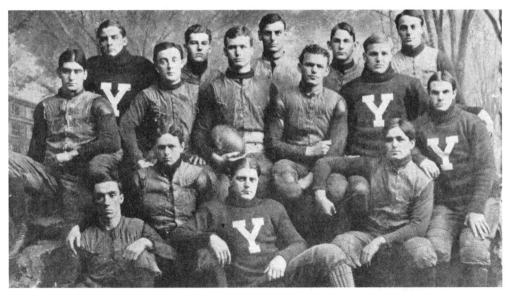

Yale's 1900 team was called the "Team of the Century" for many reasons. Captained by Francis Gordon Brown (holding the ball), the Bulldogs went 12-0 en route to a national championship, outscoring their opponents 336-10. The Elis capped the season with a 28-0 victory over Harvard. Seven players earned first team All-America honors: tackle James Bloomer (first row, third from left), Brown, halfback George Chadwick (far right), quarterback Bill Fincke (third row, right), fullback Perry Hale (second row, fourth from left), center Herman Olcott (first row, fourth from left), and tackle George Stillman (second row, fifth from left).

Yale University's bicentennial in 1901 brought some of its greatest football players back to Yale Field. Captained by Walter Camp (holding ball), the Yale alumni team took on a team of varsity substitutes on October 22, 1901. Camp kicked off, then watched from the sideline as his fellow former Elis dominated. "From the moment of the first scrimmage it became evident that the same surprising skill remained in the great players who had once brought victory to Yale," wrote the *New York Times*. The alumni won, 12-0.

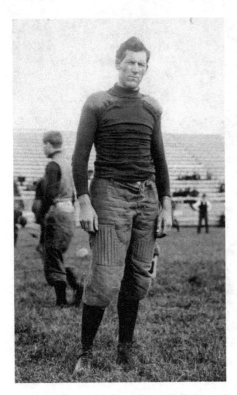

All-America guard Edgar "Ned" Glass came to Yale from Mercersburg Academy but had played at Syracuse before that. Midway through the 1901 season Harvard pointed out that Glass should not have been allowed to play, as Yale required transfers to sit out a year. The Bulldogs sat him for the Princeton and Harvard games, beating the Tigers but falling to the Cantabs. Glass returned in 1902 to help Yale to an 11-0-1 record that included a 23-0 win over Harvard.

Captain George Chadwick (left, with Charles Rafferty) of the 1902 team was having trouble sleeping as the Princeton game loomed. Trainer Mike Murphy instructed the halfback to meet him at the corner of College and Chapel Streets one morning. "There he was with a horse and buggy and a rifle for me," Chadwick told the *New York Times*. "We drove out to the country, where we saw nothing to shoot. That didn't matter. All Mike sought was a change in environment." Chadwick scored both touchdowns as Yale beat Princeton 12-5.

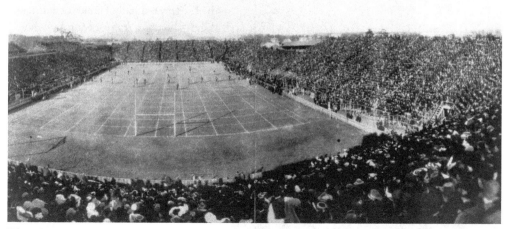

The 1903 season included a historic occasion, as Thomas Edison captured the Yale-Princeton game on film. It also saw a key rule change. To open up the game, the back that first received the snap was allowed to run with the ball between the 25-yard lines as long as he was five yards on either side of center when he crossed the line of scrimmage. In 1904, the rule was extended to include the areas inside the 25-yard lines. The field was thus marked with longitudinal lines, giving it a checkerboard appearance. In 1910, backs were allowed to cross the line of scrimmage at any point and the field returned to its familiar gridiron look.

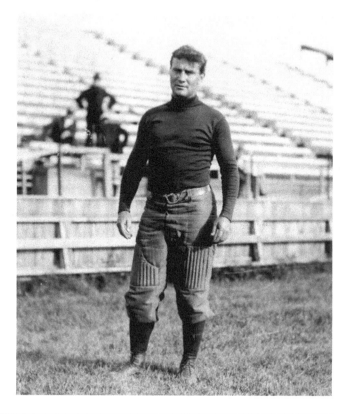

Born in Glenbane, Tipperary, tackle Jim Hogan was one of the leaders of Yale's "Irish Line" at the beginning of the 20th century that also included end Charles Rafferty, tackle Ralph Kinney, guard Ned Glass, center Henry Holt, guard George Goss, and end Tom Shevlin. The captain in 1904, he was so closely identified with the team that his nickname was "Yale." A three-time All-American, Hogan was elected to the College Football Hall of Fame in 1954.

Mike Murphy (right, with Jim Hogan in 1904) was a hall of famer of a unique kind—he was a trainer. Murphy, who was inducted into the National Athletic Trainer's Association Hall of Fame in 1962, was renowned for his work with both the football team and the track team. He started at Yale in 1888 and was a key part of the team's success at the beginning of the 20th century.

An All-American at halfback in 1903, Ledyard Mitchell went on to help organize the Chrysler Corporation in 1925. The award for Yale's best kicker is named in his honor. (From the 1904 *Yale Pot-Pourri*.)

Foster Rockwell (receiving snap, with Tad Jones to his right) was a two-time All-American at quarterback for Yale. From 1902 to 1904, he helped the Bulldogs to a 32-2-1 record. He coached the team to a 9-0-1 mark in 1906.

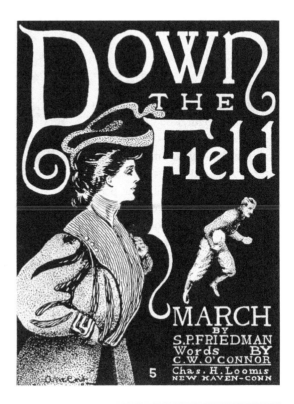

The 1900s marked the debut of classic Yale songs "Boola Boola" and "Bright College Years" at football games. In 1904, "Down the Field" came on the scene in the 12-0 win at Princeton. It was composed by Stanleigh Friedman and written by C. W. O'Connor.

Hall of fame end Tom Shevlin, son of a wealthy lumberman from Minnesota, was known for his confidence and ferociousness on the field and his generosity off it. A three-time first team All-American at end, he captained Yale to a 10-0 mark in 1905 and a share of the national championship.

Hall of fame brothers Howard (left, an end) and Thomas Albert Dwight "Tad" Jones (right, a quarterback) helped the Elis to a 28-0-2 record and three national championships from 1905 to 1907. They went on to careers as coaches. Howard spent two seasons at Yale but earned his fame at the University of Southern California, where his teams won four national titles. Tad compiled a 60-15-4 mark in 10 years at Yale (1916–1917, 1920–1927). He famously told his team in 1923, "Gentlemen, you are now going to play football against Harvard. Never again in your whole life will you do anything as important."

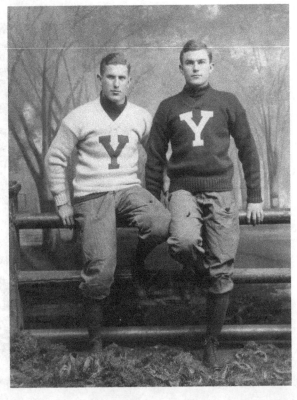

As the injuries in college football games mounted it became clear that a change was needed. Walter Camp (left, with William Knox) was among those summoned by Pres. Theodore Roosevelt in October 1905 to come up with a solution to the violence that plagued the game. That led to a meeting of 28 colleges in New York and the formation of the National Collegiate Athletic Association. In January 1906, the legalization of the forward pass was one of many measures adopted to open up the game.

Harvard Stadium was the site for what was billed as the "Battle of the Giants" in 1909—9-0 Yale against 8-0 Harvard. The Bulldogs had not allowed a point all year, amassing 201 themselves. Harvard had outscored its foes 103-9 and had an 18-game unbeaten streak. A punt block by center Carroll Cooney gave Yale a safety and a 2-0 lead. Fullback Ted Coy added two field goals for the 8-0 final that crowned Yale as national champions. (Courtesy of Walter Camp Papers, Manuscripts and Archives, Yale University Library.)

"Football enthusiasts, grown up as well as youngster, found in Ted Coy the living image of what they thought a Yale football hero should look like," wrote Tim Cohane in the *Yale Football Story*. Coy was a three-time All-American and a hall of famer at fullback, and he scored both touchdowns in Yale's come-from-behind 12-10 win over Princeton in 1907. In 1909, an operation to remove his appendix kept him out of the first four games. He returned to captain Yale to another national title and a 10-0 record. (Courtesy of Library of Congress, Prints and Photographs Division, LC-DIG-ggbain-04340.)

After the 1908 season, it was discovered that guard Ham Andrus had played the Harvard game with a broken bone in his arm. He was an All-American that year and again in 1909. Andrus went on to a successful career as a financier, earning the nickname "millionaire strap hanger" because of his frequent use of the subway.

Hall of famer John Reed Kilpatrick was an All-America end in 1909 and 1910. Kilpatrick was a colonel in World War I and a brigadier general in World War II. After leaving the Army, he eventually became president and then chairman of the board of Madison Square Garden. He was also president of the NHL's New York Rangers.

The quarterback on Yale's legendary 1909 team was 5-foot-10-inch, 153-pound sophomore Art Howe. The following season Howe accounted for the decisive score against Princeton. His touchdown pass to John Reed Kilpatrick gave Yale the 5-3 upset (touchdowns were increased to six points two years later). Howe earned All-America status in 1911, including a game against Princeton in which he set a collegiate record by returning 18 kicks. He was elected to the College Football Hall of Fame in 1973.

Despite injuries, Douglass Bomeisler was an All-American at end in 1911 and 1912. He was hurt in the second game of the 1910 season and missed the rest of that year. He played through the 1911 season with a dislocated shoulder. He also injured his right knee against Princeton that year but invented a knee brace that enabled him to continue playing. Bomeisler was elected to the College Football Hall of Fame in 1972.

Hall of famer Henry "Hank" Ketcham earned All-America honors while developing the "roving center" technique on defense. Instead of playing on the line, Ketcham played back two or three yards to gain a better view of the play. As captain in 1913, Ketcham announced Howard Jones as Yale's first salaried coach after a graduate committee recognized the need for a change in Yale's coaching structure.

Archibald MacLeish lettered for Yale in 1913 before embarking on a Pulitzer Prize-winning writing career. "Conventional wisdom notwithstanding, there is no reason either in football or in poetry why the two should not meet in a man's life if he has the weight and cares about the words," he wrote in "Moonlighting on Yale Field," *Riders on Earth*.

All-America tackle Nelson "Bud" Talbott lettered from 1912 to 1914, captaining the team to a 7-2 record as a senior. His grandson Dave became the Yale men's squash coach in 1984 and led the Bulldogs to national championships in 1989 and 1990. His grandson Mark coached the Yale women's squash team from 1998 through 2004, winning a national title in his final season. Dave Talbott began coaching the women after his brother left and led them to two more national championships.

One estimate in the early 1900s had Yale missing out on $100,000 in ticket sales because of the limited seating capacity at Yale Field. The Alumni Advisory Board recommended a new stadium, and formed a "Committee of 21" to oversee the project. The committee's recommendations included permanent fireproof stands and a capacity of no less than 60,000. Charles Ferry, an 1871 Yale graduate, proposed a unique design that would ensure the stadium's permanence; he would build it by digging a hole in the ground for the field, placing seating on the displaced earth surrounding the hole. In June 1913, at the site just across Derby Avenue from Yale Field, Yale president Arthur Twining Hadley turned the ceremonial first sod. Yale's new field would be 27 feet below ground, with 30 tunnels through the stands for spectators.

3

THE BOWL

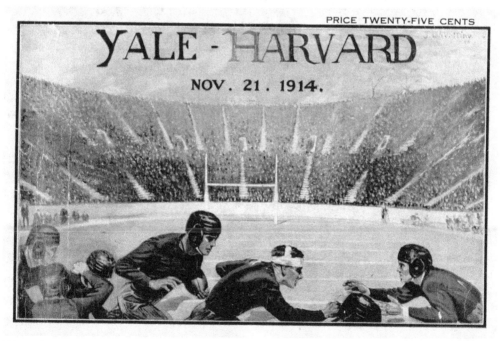

The Yale Bowl opened on November 21, 1914, for Yale's game with Harvard, hosting a crowd of 70,000. The New Haven Railroad needed 43 special trains, carrying an estimated 30,000 people, to accommodate the mob that descended on New Haven. There were 150 trolley cars in action to get people to and from the game.

After Yale's Harry LeGore fielded the opening kickoff and returned it 30 yards, the first game at the Yale Bowl belonged to Harvard. The final was 36-0, a payback for the result the first time Harvard hosted Yale in Harvard Stadium 11 years earlier—12-0 Yale. (Photograph by Candee; courtesy of photograph collection of Brian K. Welch, class of 1916, Yale College, documenting life at Yale and in New Haven, c. 1916, Manuscripts and Archives, Yale University Library.)

Tom Shevlin never failed to respond when Yale needed him. He was called upon to help coach for the Princeton game in 1915. "The only sound that broke the silence was the nervous shuffling of cleats on the stone floor," wrote senior Wayne Chatfield-Taylor of the atmosphere before the game. "All eyes were fixed on the broad back of the coach as he paced up and down. Suddenly he turned on the waiting group: 'What do we do to-day?' he shouted. 'Hold the ball!' was his enthusiastic answer. 'What do we do when we tackle?' 'We tackle!' 'All right, boys, you're going out there now and fight for yourselves first, then for the University, and then, if you care at all, for the old man—I'm through now, it's up to you!' His voice broke with the last words, then as tears ran down his cheeks, with a quick smile he yelled triumphantly, 'What do we do to-day?' And as the team rose to its feet, 'Hold the ball!' echoed louder than before." Yale beat Princeton 13-7. Tragically, Shevlin would catch pneumonia and pass away just over a month later. Chatfield-Taylor's words appeared in a special book published in Shevlin's memory. (Courtesy of Manuscripts and Archives, Yale University Library.)

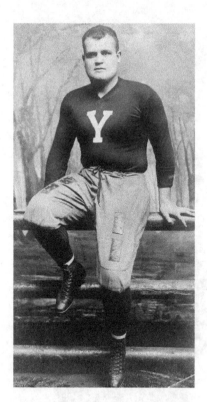

As team captain in 1916, guard Clinton "Cupe" Black had the distinction of wearing No. 1 when the Elis added numbers to their uniforms that year. Black earned All-America status, leading Yale to an 8-1 record.

Chester "Chet" LaRoche quarterbacked Yale in 1916 before serving as a lieutenant in the Navy in World War I. He returned to play one more year in 1919. He went on to a career in advertising and was the first president, and later chairman of the board, of the National Football Foundation and College Football Hall of Fame, Inc. Yale's annual award for the senior who "by his character, academic talents and concern for others, did the most for Yale" is named after LaRoche.

Yale's record stood at 7-1 and Harvard's was 7-2 as the rivals met on November 25, 1916, at the Yale Bowl. The Bulldogs were seeking their first win over the Cantabs since 1909. Harvard took a 3-0 lead in the first, but Yale tackle Artemus Gates ran a Yale fumble to the Harvard 12 to set up a touchdown run by halfback Joe Neville in the second quarter. That was all the scoring in the 6-3 win. A crowd of 77,000 was on hand for what turned out to be the end of an era. War was raging in Europe, and within five months the United States joined the Allies' battle. Yale played an abbreviated three-game schedule in 1917, and the entire 1918 season was cancelled. Yale and Harvard would not meet again until 1919. (Courtesy of Manuscripts and Archives, Yale University Library.)

Among the casualties of World War I was quarterback Alex Wilson, the captain of the 1915 team. On September 29, 1918, Wilson was commanding Company A, 59th Infantry, 8th Brigade northwest of Verdun in France as part of the Argonne offensive. A German bullet pierced his right arm above the elbow, but he refused to fall back for first aid. Later in the morning he was shot in the head and killed instantly. "And true he was a man of men," wrote a sergeant from Wilson's company in *Yale in the World War*, "one who always would use the best of judgment about all things and one who would take his mess kit and eat what his men did and take only the same portion they did."

Malcolm Aldrich's all-around game made him an All-American in 1921. The halfback scored 87 points in nine games, captaining the Bulldogs to an 8-1 record. He also excelled on defense and at punting and kicked two fourth-quarter field goals in Yale's 13-7 win over Princeton.

Yale won the first two games of the 1923 season, against North Carolina and Georgia, by a combined score of 93-0. That set the tone for a dominant season. Wins over Bucknell and Brown followed, then a 31-10 victory over Army. After surviving a scare from Maryland, 16-14, Yale finished off its undefeated season with wins over Princeton (27-0) and Harvard (13-0).

ELI BRILLIANT IN BIG TRIUMPH OVER ARMY

When Eagle-Eyed Blair Pounced on Fumble by Cadet Wood and Scampered Over West Point's Goal Line During First Half of Stirring Game at Bowl

Elusive Smythe-Snapped as He Got Off to Spectacular 70 Yard Dash That Gave the Army Its Lone Touchdown

POWER AND PUNCH BRING 31 TO 10 WIN

Bulldog Tenacity Denotes Sensational Dashes of Speedy Chiefs, Backs and Rolls Heavy Score in First Half—Neidlinger, Stevens, Blair, Neale and Smythe Star.

Martial Splendor Of Cadets' Drill Held Crowd Spellbound

NO ACCIDENTS DESPITE BIG TRAFFIC JAMS

BANKERS SHOW KEEN INTEREST IN GERMAN LOAN

Plurality Of 2,500 For FitzGerald Is Aim Of Democrats Tuesday

CROWN PRINCE IS SICK ABED AT WIERINGEN

The largest crowd in the history of the Yale Bowl, 80,000 people jammed the stands for the 1923 Army game. Tackle Ted Blair recovered a fumble forced by fullback Bill Mallory for a touchdown in the second quarter for a 7-3 lead, but Army went back ahead on a punt return for a touchdown. Yale took the lead for good on a fake kick that resulted in a touchdown pass from halfback Widdy Neale to end Richard Luman in the third quarter. The final was 31-10. (Courtesy of New Haven Register.)

The award for Yale's most valuable player is named after Edwin Foster "Ted" Blair. A tackle on Yale's 1923 team that had a record of 8-0, Blair also got a law degree and an honorary master's degree from Yale. His many roles with his alma mater included serving as a member of the Yale Corporation and as the founder and president of the Yale Football Y Association. When he passed away, former teammate Ducky Pond said "I never had known a finer man than Ted Blair—his hobby was doing kind things for people."

Yale's William Neely Mallory Award is presented annually to the senior male athlete who "on the field of play, and in his life at Yale, best represents the highest ideals of American sportsmanship and Yale tradition." It honors "Memphis Bill" Mallory, an All-America fullback who captained Yale's undefeated 1923 team and earned election to the College Football Hall of Fame in 1964. Mallory was a Major in the Air Force during World War II and received the Legion of Merit Medal for "Operation Mallory," a plan that cut 22 of the 24 bridges over the River Po in Italy and seriously hampered German movement. Scheduled for release, Mallory was one of 10 people killed February 19, 1945, when their transport plane crashed while taking off from an Italian field.

Halfback William "Widdy" Neale was a member of Yale's undefeated 1923 team. He returned to his alma mater in 1933 to head up the intramural program, also coaching the freshman team. In 1951, he was promoted to business manager. Also the golf coach, Neale led Yale to a national title in 1943. His brother, hall of famer Earle "Greasy" Neale, was an assistant coach at Yale and head coach of the Philadelphia Eagles.

Hall of fame tackle Century Milstead's birth date—January 1, 1901—explained his unique first name. As a transfer to Yale from Wabash College, Milstead was ineligible to play in the 1922 season. Legend has it that when the six-foot-four-inch, 220-pounder made back-to-back tackles for a loss in a scrimmage that year he was ordered to the sidelines so he would not hurt anyone. Milstead earned All-America honors in 1923.

Sportswriter Grantland Rice called hall of famer Marvin "Mal" Stevens one of the best running backs he had ever seen. Stevens transferred to Yale from Washburn, helping the Elis go 8-0 in 1923. He succeeded Tad Jones as head coach in 1928. After receiving his medical degree he scaled back his duties in 1933, coaching just the freshmen, and became an instructor in orthopedic surgery. He left in 1934 to coach and teach at New York University, and also was team physician for the New York Yankees.

Hall of famer Herbert "Cobbles" Sturhahn was an All-American at guard in 1925 and 1926 after taking on a starting role as a sophomore. Yale went 15-6-3 in his three years with the varsity.

"Bruising" Bruce Caldwell was a key part of Yale's attack at halfback from 1925 to 1927, earning selection to the Shrine East-West game in 1927. The Bulldogs were national champions that year with a 7-1 record. Caldwell also starred for the Yale baseball team and played 18 games with the Cleveland Indians in 1928. He returned to New Haven to play for the Profs, a local professional baseball team, the following year.

Walter Camp traveled to New York to attend the meeting of the Intercollegiate Football Rules Committee on March 13, 1925. After a late session, he returned to his room in the Hotel Belmont. When he did not show up for a 9:30 meeting the next morning, his colleagues sent Princeton coach Bill Roper and committee member W. S. Langford to investigate. They entered Camp's room and found him in his bed, where he had died of a heart attack. "What Washington was to his country, Camp was to American football—the friend, the founder and the father," said legendary coach John Heisman.

4

THE AGE OF THE
IRON MEN

Following Walter Camp's death, Yale sought a suitable way to pay tribute to him. The Walter Camp Memorial Gateway leading to the Yale Bowl from Derby Avenue was dedicated on November 3, 1928, at Yale's 18-0 win over Dartmouth. It was erected through contributions from alumni of Yale and from 224 other colleges and 279 preparatory and high schools.

On December 30, 1928, guard Norman Hall was skating with his friend's sister on a frozen lake when the ice gave way and both fell into the water. Hall held the girl above water and she was able to be rescued, but the frigid conditions took their toll on him and he sank before his own rescue was possible. Yale's Norman S. Hall Award is given to an individual for "outstanding service to Yale football."

Tackle Francis T. "Fay" Vincent captained Yale to a 5-2-2 mark in 1930. Vincent also captained the baseball team at Yale, and his son Francis T. "Fay" Vincent Jr. went on to become Major League Baseball commissioner. (From the 1931 *Yale Banner and Pot Pourri.*)

THE AGE OF THE IRON MEN

New Haven fans had a local to cheer for during the Depression, as halfback Albie Booth moved from Hillhouse High to Milford Prep to Yale. The five-foot-seven-inch, 144-pound dynamo announced his presence in the 1929 game against Army at the Yale Bowl. With the Elis trailing 13-0, Booth ran for two touchdowns and kicked two extra points, then returned a punt for a touchdown (giving him 223 yards for the day) and the 21-13 final. Attracting nicknames such as "Little Boy Blue," "The Mighty Atom," and more, he led Yale to a 15-5-5 mark from 1929 through 1931, rushing for 1,428 yards and adding 1,138 yards on kick returns. His field goal against Harvard in 1931 won the game for Yale, 3-0. He would go on to earn enshrinement in the College Football Hall of Fame in 1966.

Among the means of providing unemployment relief during the Depression was a charity football tournament December 5, 1931, at the Yale Bowl. It started with two 24-minute games, one between Holy Cross and Yale and one between Brown and Dartmouth. The Bulldogs beat Holy Cross 6-0 on a Joe Crowley touchdown. The Yale-Brown match up for the championship ended in a scoreless tie, with Yale declared the winner through a point system based on criteria such as yards gained. More than $45,000 was raised.

Former Eli Amos Alonzo Stagg (right) won 314 games at the International YMCA Training School (now Springfield College), the University of Chicago, and the College of the Pacific during a 54-year coaching career. Known as the "Grand Old Man of the Midway" for his exploits at Chicago, Stagg returned to New Haven in 1932 to coach the "Monsters of the Midway" to a 7-7 tie with Yale. (Photograph by International Newsreel; courtesy of Manuscripts and Archives, Yale University Library.)

THE AGE OF THE IRON MEN

Raymond "Ducky" Pond, shown here with Handsome Dan II, succeeded Dr. Marvin Stevens as head coach in 1934. Pond earned his nickname as a player in the 1923 Harvard game, when he ran for the only touchdown on a field drenched with rain. After accumulating a 30-25-2 win-loss record, he moved on to coach at Bates and serve in the U.S. Navy during World War II. (Photograph by Robert B. Silleck; courtesy of Manuscripts and Archives, Yale University Library.)

End John Hersey lettered for the football team in 1934 and 1935, but his future was more apparent from the fact that he wrote for the *Yale Daily News*. He went on to a Pulitzer Prize-winning career as an author and journalist.

Princeton was 6-0 on the season and had 15 wins in a row overall when Yale came to town on November 17, 1934. The Tigers had outscored their opponents 242-18 and the Bulldogs were heavy underdogs. In front of a crowd of 52,000 at Palmer Stadium a great drama played out. Before the game, Princeton coach Fritz Crisler lined his team up practically from goal line to goal line. In contrast, Yale's traveling roster included just 28 men. Only 11 of them would be needed. The Bulldogs took a 7-0 lead in the first quarter on a 43-yard pass from Jerry Roscoe to Larry Kelley (shown below). Princeton drove to the Yale five-yard line in the second quarter but the Bulldogs stuffed four runs. After that the main question was whether the Elis' starting 11 could finish the entire 60-minute game without substitution. They did. The feat, which has never been repeated in major college football, earned them the nickname "Iron Men." Seen above, they were, from left to right, as follows: (first row) end Larry Kelley, tackle Jack Wright, guard Ben Grosscup, center Jim DeAngelis, guard Clare Curtin, tackle Meredith Scott, and end Robert "Choo Choo" Train; (second row) halfback Strat Morton, fullback Kim Whitehead, quarterback Jerry Roscoe, and halfback Stan Fuller. (Bottom photograph by Acme.)

One of the heroes of the "Iron Men" game, hall of fame end Larry Kelley went on to even greater achievements. He captained Yale to a 7-1 record in 1936, including a 26-23 win over Princeton and a 14-13 win over Harvard. He scored a touchdown in each of those games, and had the distinction of scoring a touchdown in all six "Big Three" games in his varsity career. He earned the Heisman Trophy that year.

Prior to serving as U.S. senator for Wisconsin from 1957 to 1989, William Proxmire was a football player—and a boxer—at Yale. He lettered in 1937.

Hall of fame halfback Clint Frank brought Yale its second consecutive Heisman Trophy in 1937. A great player on both sides of the ball, Frank captained the Bulldogs to a 6-1-1 record, running for 190 yards and four touchdowns in a 26-0 win over Princeton. His defensive performance in a loss at Harvard the next week was equally impressive, as some accounts had him making as many as 50 tackles despite an injured knee. He also broke up two potential touchdown passes, but the Crimson prevailed 13-6. Frank eschewed a chance to play professionally after graduation and joined an advertising firm. He eventually had his own firm, Clinton E. Frank Inc., and was involved in numerous charitable causes. He remained generous to his alma mater, and his many contributions included Clint Frank Field—home to Yale's junior varsity team. (Photograph by Terri Altieri, New Haven Register.)

Yale's 1938 coaching staff included Jim DeAngelis (left), one of Yale's "Iron Men" who upset Princeton 7-0 in 1934. DeAngelis's fellow coaches included Ivan "Ivy" Williams (center) and a Yale law school student, Gerald Ford (right). Ford, who had played football at Michigan, passed up professional offers to come to Yale as a coach and get his law degree. He went on to become the 38th president of the United States.

Center Spencer Moseley played much of the 1941 season with a broken jaw. The following year he captained Yale to its first Big Three championship (wins over Harvard and Princeton) in six years. His father, George, had been an All-America end on Yale's 1916 team that had an 8-1 record. Spencer made 19 tackles against Harvard in his senior year despite a broken finger and an injured knee. Like his father, he earned All-America recognition. He went on to serve as a Marine pilot in World War II and in Korea.

The circumstances of World War II led Wayne Johnson Jr. to a unique achievement. Johnson was a fullback at Harvard in 1942 and played against Yale in a 7-3 Bulldog win. He then enlisted in the Marine Corps and found himself assigned to officer candidate training at Yale, where he was eligible to play for the Elis. He was injured on his first carry, temporarily paralyzed after fracturing his neck. He recovered to attend Yale's football banquet in December, where the Harvard man received his Yale letter—the only man to earn football letters from both schools. (Photograph by Samuel Kravitt.)

5

A F T E R T H E W A R

World War II decimated rosters and schedules throughout college football—Yale did not play Harvard or Princeton in 1944. Still, coach Howard Odell got the most out of a squad that consisted mainly of servicemen who had never played and civilian freshmen. He switched to the T formation to make better use of his personnel. Yale was 6-0 when it took on the teams that replaced Princeton and Harvard on the schedule. The Bulldogs beat North Carolina 13-6 and tied Virginia 6-6 to complete their first undefeated season since 1924. (Photograph by Samuel Kravitt.)

Marlin "Buzzy" Gher was an Air Medal-winning aerial gunner in the South Pacific in 1942 and 1943, then played halfback on Yale's undefeated 1944 team. Gher's magnetic personality resonated with the local youths, inspiring the formation of "Buzzy Gher fan clubs."

An All-America end in 1944, Paul Walker (left, with Pudge Heffelfinger) also starred in basketball (he was captain of Yale's 14-4 1944–1945 squad) and baseball. He captained Yale to a 6-3 record on the gridiron in 1945, including wins over Princeton and Harvard. (Courtesy of Manuscripts and Archives, Yale University Library.)

Art Fitzgerald scored three touchdowns against Harvard in 1945, tying an 1884 record for touchdowns against Yale's rival. The Bulldogs' 28-0 win that day represented their first shutout of Harvard in 11 years, and the largest margin of victory for Yale in the series since winning by the same score in 1900. (Courtesy of New Haven Register.)

Tackle John Prchlik left for active naval duty midway through the 1944 season. Following service as an ensign in the South Pacific, he returned in 1946. The biggest Bulldog at six-feet-four-inches, 215 pounds, he presented a formidable figure and merited a spot in the Shrine East-West game in 1948. He went on to spend five seasons in the NFL. (Photograph by Samuel Kravitt.)

Fritz Barzilauskas was shot down over Sinzig while with the Army Air Forces and captured by the Nazis. Freed by the 13th American Armored Division, he joined Yale in 1945 and became a top lineman. He played professionally with the Boston Yanks for two seasons before moving on to the New York Bulldogs and the New York Giants. Injuries forced him to retire and he returned to Yale as an assistant football coach.

Lineman Bill Schuler played a season at Auburn before entering the service in 1943. He was shot down over a Messerschmitt factory and was a prisoner of war. Upon his return to the United States he enrolled at Yale and earned letters for the Bulldogs in 1945 and 1946. He played two seasons in the NFL.

Trolleys were the main method of transportation to Yale football games for decades, eventually giving way to buses and cars. The last year for the open trolleys was 1947. (Photograph by Kent Cochrane; courtesy of George Baehr Collection, Shore Line Trolley Museum Library, East Haven.)

Herman Hickman (left) arrived as Yale's head coach in 1948. His personality was as distinctive as his 300-plus-pound frame; he had wrestled professionally as "the Tennessee Terror," he enjoyed poetry, and he loved to top off his meals with a Ramon Allones cigar. Here he "coaches" New York restaurateur Toots Shor (standing) along with New York Yankees Tommy Henrich (crouching at left) and Yogi Berra (crouching at center) and actor Don Ameche (crouching at right). The "center" is Yale's sports information director, Charley Loftus.

The influx of former GIs on the Yale roster after World War II included Levi Jackson, a local who had starred for Hillhouse High with former Bulldog Reginald Root as his coach. Jackson earned third team All-America status his freshman year, and would lead Yale in rushing three out of four years. Following the 1948 season, he was one of the prime candidates for the following season's captaincy, putting his teammates in a position to make history. "I asked myself over and over: 'Do I want to vote for Levi, subconsciously even, just to prove I'm democratic?'" said quarterback Stu Tisdale in the *Yale Football Story*. "I wrestled with it. Finally, I worked it out. Levi deserved the captaincy, so I was going to vote for him." So did a majority of the Bulldogs, making Jackson the team's first African American captain.

Fittingly for a university that counts the father of American football, Walter Camp, among its alums, Yale has had over 100 graduates go on to coach college teams. Quarterback Charlie Ewart (right) chose a different level. He served as an assistant coach and general manager with the Philadelphia Eagles, working alongside former Yale assistant coach Greasy Neale to lead them to an NFL championship in 1948. In 1949, he took over as coach of an NFL franchise in New York known, appropriately, as the Bulldogs. His players included former Elis Art Fitzgerald (left), John Prchlik (second from left), and Fritz Barzilauskas (third from left). (Courtesy of New Haven Register.)

Fullback Bob Spears earned the Lowe Award as the outstanding player in New England in 1950. Spears's father, Clarence, a hall of famer and coach at Dartmouth, wanted him to play end, but Yale's need for a fullback prevailed. "Yes, I'd rather throw a hard block than almost any other maneuver in the game," Spears told the *Boston American*.

Most of the Bush family's athletic exploits at Yale came on the diamond. George H. W. Bush followed in the footsteps of his father, Prescott, and served as baseball captain in 1948, and George W. Bush had a brief stint with the freshman team in the 1960s. But Jonathan Bush—George H. W.'s brother—came through on the gridiron. He kicked the game-winning extra point against Holy Cross in the Elis' 14-13 win in 1950. (Photograph by Samuel Kravitt.)

The 1951 *Yale College Class Book* noted that "We had arrived as non-Communists; we walked out fiercely anti-Communist." That was the atmosphere in which lineman John Downey went to work for the CIA upon graduation. Downey was captured while on a mission in 1952 and presumed dead for two years. Imprisoned for over two decades by the Chinese government, he was released in 1973. He went on to law school and became a judge of the superior court of Connecticut. (Photograph by Samuel Kravitt.)

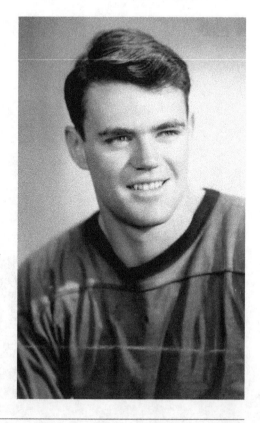

Jordan Olivar was hired as assistant coach in the spring of 1952. With Herman Hickman's sudden departure for a career in radio and television, Olivar was promoted to head coach in August. He would go on to lead Yale to a 61-32-6 record in 11 seasons, including two Ivy League championships and Yale's last undefeated, untied season (1960, 9-0).

A great two-way player, guard Dick Polich played the full 60 minutes of Yale's 7-7 tie with Colgate in 1953. He earned the Mallory award as Yale's top senior male athlete. A substitution rule change by the NCAA that year limited platooning, though still no team matched Yale's substitution-free "Iron Men" win over Princeton in 1934. Over the next several years the substitution rules were relaxed once again and platooning resumed in full force.

Charlie Yeager got to live out every Yale football manager's dream in 1952. He filled out an eligibility card on a lark at the start of the season, and the coaching staff joked that he would get into a game. Yeager was in civilian clothes at the start of the Harvard game, but he dressed for the second half as the Bulldogs began piling up points. When Yale scored its fifth touchdown head coach Jordan Olivar surveyed his bench for those who had not yet made it into the game. "The next time we score, you'll go in," he told Yeager. Shortly thereafter Ed Molloy and future Yale athletic director Ed Woodsum connected on a 57-yard touchdown, and Yeager came on to catch a pass for the point after—Yale's final point in the 41-14 win.

Yale's 1953 trip to Cornell marked the first time a Yale team had ever flown to a game. The Bulldogs came back from Ithaca with a scoreless tie. The trip was detailed in photographs in the Yale-Harvard game program that year.

Jordan Olivar (center) poses with two of his biggest offensive threats. End Ed Woodsum (left) set a Yale record with three touchdown catches in a game—twice in a span of seven games in 1952. Quarterback Ed Molloy (right) showed remarkable resiliency throughout his career, particularly in 1953. After a knee injury kept him out of the first seven games, Molloy limped onto the field with Yale trailing Princeton 17-0. The inspired Bulldogs pulled out a 26-24 win.

After lettering in 1953, guard Charles Johnson served in the U.S. Army. Now the chairman of the board of Franklin Templeton Investments, Johnson has remained committed to his alma mater. Among other gifts, he donated Charles B. Johnson '54 Field, used primarily by Yale's field hockey and lacrosse teams. His leadership gift for the renovation of Yale Bowl in 2004, matched by the class of 1954, was a major factor in moving that project forward.

Tackle William Lovejoy was one of Yale's pleasant surprises in 1954, earning a starting spot after being hampered by injuries the previous year. Also a lacrosse star, Lovejoy earned Yale's Mallory Award as the top senior male athlete in 1956. His father, Winslow, was an All-America center and captained Yale in 1924.

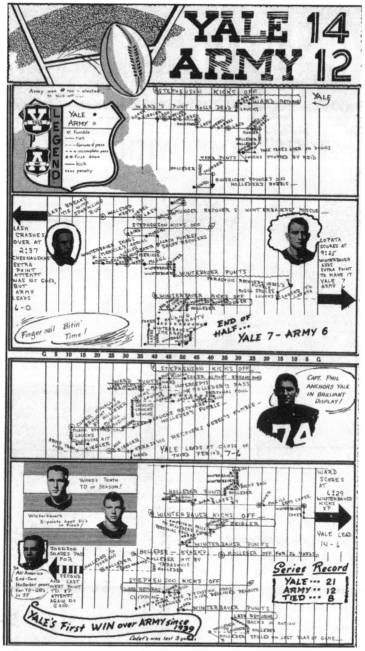

The 1955 Yale-Army game, diagrammed here in the *Football Y News*, would go down as one of the most memorable ones. The Cadets were heavily favored and had handled Yale 48-7 the previous year. With over 60,000 on hand at the Yale Bowl, tackle Phil Tarasovic recovered a Cadet fumble at the 10-yard line to set up a Dean Loucks-to-Paul Lopata touchdown for a 7-6 Yale lead at the half. The Bulldogs went up 14-6 on an Al Ward touchdown run with 8:31 remaining. Army scored to pull within two shortly thereafter, but its final drive could not get past midfield. It was the Bulldogs' first win in the series since 1939.

Prior to the 1955 season, captain Phil Tarasovic asked his father which game ball he would like. The elder Tarasovic said Army. "I know it's a big order," he said. "But that's the ball I want." Tarasovic's two fumble recoveries—part of a seven-turnover day for the Eli defense—enabled him to race to the stands after the 14-12 win and grant his father's wish.

The idea of a football league among eastern institutions had been bandied about in the 1930s, and *New York Herald Tribune* writer Caswell Adams used the term "Ivy League" in 1937. Finally in 1944, with the success of D-Day leaving the promise of peace, the athletic directors at Brown, Columbia, Cornell, Dartmouth, Harvard, Penn, Princeton, and Yale devised the "Ivy Group Agreement," affirming their observance of common practices in academic standards. The agreement underwent several revisions over time, but the change made in 1954 had a lasting impact. The schools agreed to play a round-robin schedule starting in 1956.

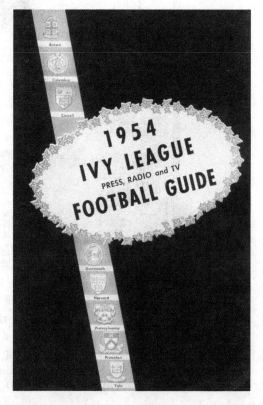

6

BIRTH OF A LEAGUE

The round-robin schedule that the Ivy League adopted in 1956 meant that was the first year that the league crowned a football champion. En route to winning that first title, Yale's 1956 team ran up 246 points—the most by a Yale team since 1903. That included 42 points against both Princeton (a 42-20 win) and Harvard (a 42-14 win). The team was captained by Mike Owseichik (holding ball) and included future hall of famer Alex Kroll (fourth row, fifth from left), who also played at Rutgers. The team also included Vern Loucks (first row, far left) and his brother Dean (first row, ninth from left). Dean led the team in passing from 1954 to 1956, while Vern went on to become Senior Fellow of the Yale Corporation.

Denny McGill (right) led Yale in rushing from 1954 through 1956, earning the Lowe Award as the outstanding player in New England as a senior. "If I can put into one word my feelings tonight, it would be grateful," McGill said at the award presentation. "I am grateful to have been a part of a great Yale team. Without the men up front, and the confidence of the players beside me, this award would not have been possible."

Denny McGill referred to fellow back Al Ward as "the greatest fellow I've ever played alongside of." In Yale's 1956 game against Harvard, with the Bulldogs' perfect league record at stake, the Crimson closed to within 14-7 midway through the second quarter when Ward came through with a backbreaking 80-yard kickoff return for a touchdown. Yale went on to win 42-14.

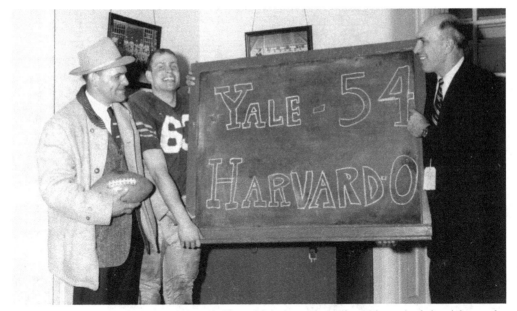

Captain Jack Embersits (second from left) and head coach Jordan Olivar (right) celebrate the team's 54-0 win over Harvard in 1957, the most points Yale has ever scored against its archrival. Back Herb Hallas scored three touchdowns, including a 58-yarder from Dick Winterbauer.

Yale added a new scoreboard in 1958, appropriately funded by the Bobby Hertz Memorial Fund. Prior to his death in 1957, Hertz was a fixture on the Yale sideline for decades in a white flannel sweater, white flannel slacks, and white shoes. He used hand signals that earned him the nickname "human semaphore" as he communicated the game's plays (down and distance, etc.) to those operating the old manual scoreboard high above the field.

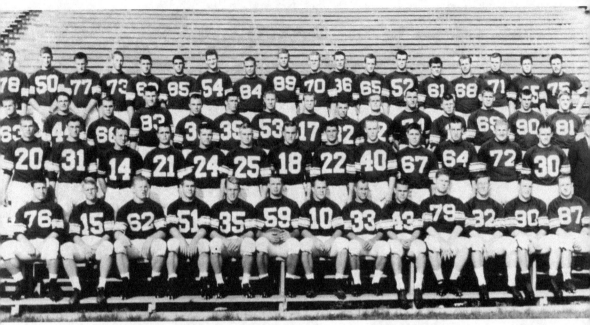

After winning the first game of the season by just three points (11-8 over UConn on a Wally Grant field goal), Yale's 1960 Ivy League championship squad began building momentum towards history. A 9-0 win over Brown followed, and then came the blowouts: 30-8 over Columbia, 22-6 over Cornell to take sole possession of first place, 36-14 over Colgate, 29-0 over Dartmouth, and 34-9 over Penn. The following 43-22 win over Princeton, who had been 5-0 in the league, marked the only time in the final five games of the season that an opponent got within three touchdowns of the Elis. They finished off the perfect season, Yale's first unbeaten and untied campaign since 1923, with a 39-6 win at Harvard. That game also marked the debut of the term "The Game" on the Yale-Harvard game program (the phrase had been used informally for years). The annual meeting between the two rivals is now referred to that way every year.

Mike Pyle, the captain of Yale's undefeated 1960 Ivy League championship team, was both physical and durable—he did not miss a game from high school until 1964, his fourth season in the NFL. He was an honorable mention All-American as a center in 1959 and as a tackle in 1960. Pyle spent nine seasons with the Chicago Bears.

Tom Singleton was perfectly suited for quarterback in Jordan Olivar's "belly" series of plays, mixing real plunges into the line with fake handoffs, bootlegs, and options. He endured his share of growing pains as part of Yale's 0-7 Ivy League campaign in his sophomore season, 1958, as he adjusted to the T formation. Back home in Illinois he got advice from former Bulldog All-Ivy quarterback Dick Winterbauer, who helped him master the system. Singleton threw for 108 yards (completing all eight of his attempts) and a touchdown, ran for 26 yards and a touchdown, kicked three extra points, punted three times, intercepted a pass, and added a two-point conversion pass in Yale's 38-20 win over Princeton in 1959.

THAT FIRST PLAY
IN THE HARVARD GAME

A Master Fake
From the "Belly Series"

Wolfe, Untouched, Goes
41 Yards for a Score

"It was the greatest bit of faking I have
ever seen on a football field."

— Stanley Woodward

This is a belly series play, launched from a Wing-T on the 41-yard line. Singleton (A) gives the ball to Blanchard (B) (or does he?) and the Harvard 7-man line focuses on the big fullback. However, it is noteworthy that Pyle (F), left tackle, is putting an *outside* block on Nelson (R), Harvard right tackle, and that some of Yale's center linemen are not concerned with primary blocks as they would be if Blanchard were making an honest line-buck. Kay (F), right guard, and King (G) right tackle, are on the way downfield as is Pappas (H), right end.

Pictures from
N.Y. Herald Tribune

At the last possible split second Singleton takes the ball from Blanchard's belly and gives it to Wolfe for a run at the off-tackle hole which is greatly widened as Nelson (R) starts to pull *away from* Pyle's block to get at Blanchard, instead of resisting it. Muller (D), the wingback, leads Wolfe through the gaping hole to seek the backer-up, while Hutcherson (J), left end, squares off to block out Messenbaugh (Q), Harvard's waiting right end. Blanchard's fake linebuck is so realistic that he is attracting the complete attention of five Harvard linemen: Nelson (R), right tackle; Christiansen (S), center; Gaston (T), right guard; Swinford (U), left guard; and Pillsbury (V), left tackle. The fake is perfect.

Completely bamboozled and entirely out of action, the Harvard line lies in a heap in the foreground as Blanchard goes through it for more than three yards with no blocking and *without the ball*. Nelson (R) is still not sure Blanchard doesn't have it and reaches out a hand for him. Meanwhile Wolfe (C) is cutting through the tackle as Hutcherson (J), screens out Messenbaugh (Q), the Harvard end. Muller (D) is leading Wolfe and heads to block out Repsher (Y), Harvard halfback. Pyle (F) is cheated out of his part in the play when the man he was blocking, Nelson (R), escaped to the wrong side to chase Blanchard. Wolfe is clear and away and could have gone any distance.

Ken Wolfe book-ended the undefeated 1960 season with two of its most significant plays. His kickoff return for a touchdown on the opening play of the preseason scrimmage set the tone for the year. In the finale against Harvard, Wolfe was the central figure in "The Play," Yale's first play of the game. Quarterback Tom Singleton executed a perfect fake to fullback Bob Blanchard (No. 35), withdrawing the ball at the last moment to hand it off to Wolfe (No. 43). Wolfe ran through the left side of the line, where linemen Mike Pyle and Ben Balme opened a gaping hole. Six Harvard defenders mistakenly converged on Blanchard. Wolfe ran 41 yards for a touchdown and Yale was on its way to a 39-6 win. "The Play" was illustrated using photos from the *New York Herald Tribune* in the program for the team's post-season celebration at the Biltmore in New York. (Courtesy of Hank Hallas.)

Noted for his speed and agility, Ben Balme dominated at guard for the Bulldogs during the 1960 season. His recognition as a first team All-American by the Associated Press marked the first time since 1953 that the organization had selected any Ivy League player for its first team, and the first time a Yale man had made it since the days of Clint Frank and Larry Kelley.

End Mike McCaskey lettered in 1963 and 1964 before moving on to a career in business. McCaskey, the grandson of legendary Chicago Bears coach and owner George Halas, took over the Bears when Halas passed away in 1983 and helped them to a Super Bowl title in 1986.

Back Chuck Mercein led Yale in rushing in 1963 and 1964, and the Giants picked him in the third round of the NFL draft. His most famous game came as a member of the Green Bay Packers—the 1967 NFL Championship, known as the "Ice Bowl." With the wind chill at minus 48 degrees at Lambeau Field, Mercein had a key 19-yard reception and an 18-yard run that set up Bart Starr's game-winning touchdown in the final seconds of the 21-17 win. (Photograph by Stu Whelan.)

Quarterback Ed McCarthy and two friends were headed for a skiing weekend on January 30, 1965, when the car they were in hit a snow bank and slammed into a tree. McCarthy perished in the accident. "Ed's real ability was to make the people around him better for having been in his presence," wrote Nelson A. Soltman in the *Yale Daily News*. McCarthy's brother, Rick, would emerge as a key offensive guard for the Bulldogs. In 2003, Rick's son Ed, also an offensive lineman, earned Ivy League Rookie of the Year honors.

Yale's Woody Knapp Memorial Trophy was awarded starting in 1968. Named after the former defensive back who graduated in 1965, it is given to the player "who best typifies the cheerful disposition, leadership qualities, and unselfish devotion to others that characterized Woody's life and accomplishments at Yale." A fighter pilot, Knapp was killed in the Vietnam War. (Photograph by Stu Whelan.)

A three-year letter winner from 1963 to 1965, quarterback and defensive back Tone Grant went on to become the president of Refco, one of the world's largest commodity trading companies. He was honored with the NCAA's Silver Anniversary Award in 1991. The Silver Anniversary Award recognizes former student-athletes who have distinguished themselves since completing their college athletics careers.

The New Haven Register
New Haven Journal-Courier

SPORTS

SATURDAY
NOVEMBER 23, 1963
PAGE 21

Classified · Financial
Comics · Features

Yale-Harvard Game Is Postpone[d]

By BILL AHERN
Register Staff Reporter

Out of respect for the late President John F. Kennedy, struck and killed by an assassin's bullet yesterday, Yale and Harvard universities have postponed their traditional football game originally scheduled for this afternoon in the Yale Bowl.

The joint announcement came in a simply-worded statement which carefully omitted any reference that the game was cancelled.

President Kennedy was a graduate of Harvard and in June, 1962, was awarded an Honorary Doctor of Laws degree by Yale at its commencement exercises.

The announcement that all athletic and social activities associated with THIS GAME were off came as the junior varsity and freshmen football games were drawing to a conclusion Friday. Players who participated in those games were unaware of the tragedy until informed by their coaches in the dressing rooms.

Whether the "Big" game will be played at all was a matter of conjecture last night. Yale President Kingman Brewster and Harvard President Nathan Pusey not conferred. Dr. Pusey was in New York City for a speaking engagement which was later cancelled because of the President's death.

The best Yale sources indicated that the game probably would be played either on Thursday (Thanksgiving Day) or next Saturday.

A definite statement will be made this morning, Yale's Director of Athletics DeLaney Kiphuth said shortly before 8 p.m. last night.

The Harvard varsity team, which had worked out in the Bowl yesterday afternoon, learned of the tragedy at the Lippard Field House. Later, at its pre-game headquarters in the Yale Motor Inn at Wallingford, the squad was pulled on whether or not they would like to play the game. The players were overwhelmingly for playing the contest at a later date.

A similar poll was conducted by Yale coach John Pont with the same result.

Both Pont, Yale's first-year varsity coach, and coach John Yovicsin of Harvard, were in accord that the two universities had acted wisely in postponing the classic.

Each said that they and their squads were happy to learn that the game was not cancelled, and said they hoped it would be played later.

Regardless of the decision to come today, members of both squads were told to report for practice Monday.

Yovicsin said that many of his players returned to Cambridge,

Mass., immediately. Others elected to stay at the motel. Still others left with families and friends.

The Harvard coach said: "The squad is in complete accord with the action of the university presidents and is happy that "be decision to respect the memory of the late President was a joint one. We are also pleased that the game was postponed, and not cancelled. We hope it will be played and are looking forward to a postponement date."

Speaking to members of the press in the Ray Tompkins House last night, a somber Pont said he felt that both universities had acted wisely. "It is a serious blow to the country," he explained. "It is right that this contest not be played today."

He agreed with Yovicsin and the Harvard squad that the classic, the 80th in a football series that began in 1875, be re-scheduled. He hoped that it wouldn't be played later than next Saturday.

"It would be unreasonable to ask the boys to play much later," he said.

Almost simultaneously with the shock of the news of the assassination, Yale's athletic headquarters became a beehive of action as scores at other university and college presidents and athletic heads telephoned to determine how Yale and Harvard would react in connection with their game.

The initial statement by both presidents read:

"Out of respect for the memory of our late President United States, we have decided that athletic and social events between Yale and Harvard which were scheduled for New will not take place this weekend."

The announcement set off similar reactions throughout nation where most teams were to wind up their seasons Foremost among them was the Dartmouth-Princeton game was to decide the Ivy championship. It has been reschedul Princeton next Saturday. Other Ivy battles were similarly t

A crowd of 60,000, the largest in the East this far this s was to have witnessed the Bowl struggle which was sch In all likelihood any replay will be without television be of previous commitments.

The late President prepared for Harvard at the Choate in Wallingford. He played football as a freshman at Ha but never competed as a member of the varsity. His fo U. S. Attorney General Robert Kennedy was his football lat Harvard.

The action on the game set a precedent. It was the first in the long football rivalry that a game had been post although the rivalry has been interrupted on eight occa

Eli Frosh Deadlock Harvard In 14-14 Fray

Teams Share Big 3 Title In Windup

By BOB BARTON
Register Staff Reporter

Justice received its service but missed its purpose yesterday afternoon at DeWitt Cuyler Field as the freshman football squads of Yale and Harvard careened to a 14-14 tie and deprived each other of the Ivy League and Big Three freshman titles.

The result was one appropriate to the strength of the two teams, and one befitting a fierce rivalry where the total margin of decisions in the past nine years has been but 31 points. But it was also one that brought two fine seasons to a disappointing end and left fights for varied honors in a total snarl.

The clubs, both victors over Princeton, had to share the Big

National Sports Slate Is Cut Down Across U.[S]

From AP, UPI Dispatches

Weekend sports events of all sorts across the nation have been postponed or cancelled in mourning for President Kennedy.

There were few notable exceptions but most of the sports activity throughout the country was called off after the assassination of the nation's sports-minded chief executive.

Most college football games, including the Yale-Harvard game, a spectacle seen many times by the President, will not be played.

The National Basketball Association called off its four Friday night games, but the Associated Press reports that tonight's Philadelphia at Boston game will be played.

National Hockey League President Clarence Campbell said that the league's game over the weekend would be played as scheduled.

and the final 36 holes will be played Sunday.

One college football game between North Carolina State and Wake Forest was played Friday night. Others will go on as scheduled, including: Michigan-Ohio State, Michigan State-Illinois, Nebraska - Oklahoma, Southern Methodist-B a y l o r, Texas-Texas Christian, Texas Tech-Arkansas, Auburn-Florida State and Arizona-New Mexico.

The Michigan State-Illinois game will be played despite the urging of Michigan Governor George Romney that the state university postpone the game.

By The Associated Press

The assassination of President Kennedy resulted in the postponement or cancellation of the following sports events:

FRIDAY
BOXING

New York — Television fight between Allen Thomas, Chicago, and Johnny Persol, New York.

card at Shenandoah Dow celled.

American Hockey Leag Quebec at Rochester, po Providence at Springfiel poned

'astern Hockey Leag Clinton at Philadelphia poned
Greensboro at Charlotte poned

TODAY
College Football

Harvard at Yale, postpo Boston Univ. at Boston poned
Columbia at Rutgers, po Colgate at Brown, postpo Xavier, Ohio, at Bowling postponed
Oregon State at Oregon poned until Nov. 30
Wisconsin at Minnesota poned until Nov. 30
Wisconsin at Minnesota, poned
Purdue at Indiana, postp Air Force at Colorado, poned

Friday, November 22, 1963, started out as any other Yale-Harvard weekend did: hundreds of people were in New Haven already, and the junior varsity and freshman games were under way. Then news began making its way through the crowd via transistor radios that Pres. John F. Kennedy had been shot. A score in the freshman game was greeted by silence from the crowd, with only the players on the field, who were unaware of what was going on, cheering. Back at the Yale athletic department headquarters the usual pre-game lull turned into an avalanche of phone calls. Everyone wanted to know about Saturday's game, and the answer came in a joint statement from Yale president Kingman Brewster Jr. and Harvard president Nathan Marsh Pusey: "OUT OF RESPECT FOR THE MEMORY OF THE LATE PRESIDENT OF THE UNITED STATES WE HAVE DECIDED THAT THE ATHLETIC AND SOCIAL ACTIVITIES INVOLVING HARVARD AND YALE UNIVERSITIES WHICH WERE SCHEDULED FOR NEW HAVEN SHALL NOT TAKE PLACE THIS WEEKEND." The announcement was the first of its kind to reach the news outlets that day, and soon more teams across the country followed suit. The following day it was announced that The Game would be played the following Saturday, and it was. President Kennedy himself had written, in an article that ran in the 1962 Yale-Princeton game program, that he "hoped the coming generation would continue to have the pleasure of football and learn the hard and very useful lessons which it teaches." (Courtesy of New Haven Register.)

7

VERY CAPABLE HANDS

When head coach John Pont left Yale for Indiana in January 1965, the Bulldogs went looking for a man who would add some stability to the position—the average tenure for a Yale coach at that point was around four seasons. Yale turned to one of Pont's assistants, Carm Cozza (left), naming him head coach on January 29. "The future of Yale football is in very capable hands," said athletic director DeLaney Kiphuth (right).

Bob Greenlee was half of Yale's "Jolly Green Giants" at tackle. Standing six-feet-four-inches and weighing 240 pounds, he and six-foot-two-inch, 235-pound Glenn Greenberg were a difficult combination for opposing lines to handle. Greenlee captained both the football and track teams as a senior and was drafted by the AFL's Miami Dolphins in 1966. He chose to go to Yale Law School instead.

The other half of the Jolly Green Giants, Glenn Greenberg (left), was first team All-Ivy in 1967 just as his brother Steve (right) was in soccer. Steve also lettered in baseball, the sport in which their father, Hank, made the hall of fame. (Photograph by Sabby Frinzi.)

End Mark Young (left, being "timed" by center Fred Morris) earned varsity letters in football in 1965 and 1966 before deciding to concentrate on his track career. The move paid off. Young captained the 1968 outdoor Heptagonal champion Bulldogs. He returned to his alma mater as a coach in 1980 and was named cross-country coach of the year in 1987. Young coached at the Olympics in 2000. (Photograph by Stu Whelan.)

Yale won its first eight games in 1968, extending its overall winning streak to 16. Only a 29-29 tie at Harvard in the finale spoiled the Bulldogs' bid for complete perfection, but they did claim another Ivy League title. Eight Bulldogs were named first team All-Ivy: linebacker Mike Bouscaren (first row, 11th from left), quarterback Brian Dowling (first row, holding ball), defensive back Ed Franklin (first row, 12th from left), offensive tackle Kyle Gee (first row, far left), running back Calvin Hill (second row, far left), end Del Marting (first row, far right), end Bruce Weinstein (first row, fifth from left), and middle guard Dick Williams (first row, seventh from left).

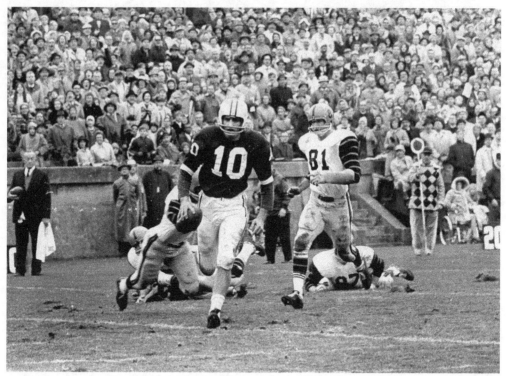

One of the first stars of the Cozza era was quarterback Brian Dowling. He made a quick impression in 1966, leading the Elis to a 16-0 win over UConn in the opener, but was injured in the first quarter of the next game. Hampered by another injury at the start of 1967, he did not take a snap until week four. He proceeded to lead the Elis to 14 straight victories over a two-season stretch, including back-to-back Ivy titles. (Photograph by Sabby Frinzi.)

Yale student Garry Trudeau based the character "B.D." in his comic strip "Bull Tales" in the *Yale Daily News* on Brian Dowling, and kept the character when the strip became the nationally syndicated "Doonesbury." In addition to the football team, Yale's decision to admit women in 1969 was also a subject for "Bull Tales." (Courtesy of Yale Daily News.)

Calvin Hill was All-Ivy and led Yale in rushing in the back-to-back Ivy League championship seasons of 1967 and 1968. He scored 14 touchdowns in 1968, earning All-East and honorable mention All-America recognition. In addition to scoring 24 touchdowns for his career, he also threw six touchdown passes. Hill was also an outstanding track performer and set the outdoor Heptagonal record in the long jump.

Jim Gallagher (center) was an honorable mention All-American at defensive end in 1969, when Yale won its third straight Ivy title, and in 1970. Defensive tackle Tom Neville (left) personified the term student-athlete. He was a member of Phi Beta Kappa, an Academic All-American, and a Rhodes Scholar. He received an NCAA Scholarship and the National Football Foundation Scholar-Athlete Award. Back Don Martin (right) went on to play in the NFL and was an assistant coach at Yale and with the Oakland Raiders.

Jack Ford was a three-year starter at defensive back. As a sophomore in 1969, he returned an interception 77 yards for a touchdown in a 21-3 win over Penn (shown here). That started a string of three straight wins at the end of the season that gave Yale a share of the Ivy League title. Ford went on to an Emmy Award-winning career in television news. (Photograph by Sabby Frinzi.)

Yale's campus was in danger of boiling over in 1970. Amidst a backdrop of protests, New Haven was the site for the murder trial of Black Panther Bobby Seale. At a faculty meeting to discuss the situation, defensive back Kurt Schmoke was given a chance to speak. Many expected him to deliver anti-establishment rhetoric. Instead he pleaded for guidance. John Hersey described the reaction in his book *Letter to the Alumni*: "Overcome by the filial courtesy and the implacable challenge of these words, the entire faculty stood and applauded Kurt as he left." Schmoke went on to become mayor of Baltimore.

VERY CAPABLE HANDS

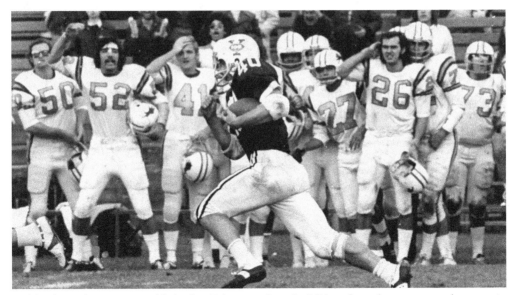

Halfback Dick Jauron established a Yale record with 962 yards rushing as a sophomore in 1970. He broke his own record with 1,055 yards in 1972, earning first team All-Ivy selection (for the third time) along with All-America status. In this photograph he takes off for an 87-yard touchdown in the fourth quarter of Yale's 28-14 win over Columbia. (Photograph by Kirby Kennedy, New Haven Register.)

Yale celebrated its football centennial in 1972. A special banquet was held at the Waldorf-Astoria in January 1973, featuring current team members and former Bulldogs. (Photograph by Sabby Frinzi.)

Brian Clarke's unique style included long hair, a brief stint at linebacker during a scrimmage, and a practice schedule that did not include his specialty—kicking—on Fridays. "Placekickers are a little different," said head coach Carm Cozza diplomatically. Clarke set a Yale record with 21 career field goals. He went on to a career in television that included roles on *General Hospital* and *Eight is Enough*. (Photograph by Sabby Frinzi.)

Tyrell "Hurricane" Hennings's (second from left) mohawk haircut drew plenty of notice at training camp in 1973. Among those admiring Hennings's hairdo was Rudy Green (left), who proved to be a key part of the Eli offensive backfield along with Hennings. Green led the team in rushing in 1973 and 1974, earning the Blair Award as team MVP on Yale's '74 Ivy League championship team. Also in the photo is Elvin Charity (right), a second team member of the Ivy League's Silver Anniversary All-Star Football Team at defensive back. (Photograph by Sabby Frinzi.)

Growing up near Bulldog great Mike Pyle in Lake Forest, Illinois, guard Greg Dubinetz came to Yale hoping to follow in Pyle's footsteps to the pros. Dubinetz was drafted by the Cincinnati Bengals in the ninth round of the 1975 NFL draft but was released after seven exhibition games. He was picked up by the Charlotte Hornets of the World Football League and played there until the league folded midway through the 1975 season. After some time in the Canadian Football League, he signed with the New York Giants as a free agent, but was cut again before playing in a game. He spent the 1978 season with the Racine Gladiators of the Northern States Football League. Finally in 1979, he realized his NFL dream. He survived the final cut with the Washington Redskins and went on to play in 15 games. Dubinetz was killed in an automobile accident in 1982, and the Bulldogs established an annual award in his honor. The Gregory Dubinetz Memorial Trophy is presented to the lineman who best exemplified Dubinetz's spirit as a player and a person.

An All-Ivy selection in 1974 and 1975 as Yale's "monster back" on defense, John Cahill's position had him lining up at various spots on the field based on field position and the strength of the opponent's formation. "The monster man is the extra man in the line, or in the backfield," Carm Cozza explained to the *New Haven Register*. "He has to be a linebacker, or a pass defender, and in a sense, a defensive end. He has to be versatile." (Photograph by Sabby Frinzi.)

Gary Fencik left Yale with just about every record a receiver could get, including 86 career catches for 1,435 yards. That included 97 yards on one reception against Princeton in 1975, a record that still stands. Fencik was picked in the 1976 NFL draft by the Miami Dolphins. He suffered a ruptured lung and was released, but the Chicago Bears picked him up. Converted to defense, Fencik went on to play for 12 seasons, including starting at free safety in the Bears' win over New England in Super Bowl XX. (Photograph by Sabby Frinzi.)

Former Bulldogs Calvin Hill and Dick Jauron pose at the 1975 Pro Bowl. A first-round pick of the Dallas Cowboys, Hill earned the rookie of the year award in 1969 and was a part of Dallas' Super Bowl VI championship. He ran for 95 yards in a game against the New York Giants at the Yale Bowl, the Giants' home for two seasons, in 1973. His son, Grant, was a first-round pick of the NBA's Detroit Pistons in 1994 and earned rookie of the year honors. Jauron was selected by the Detroit Lions in the 1973 NFL draft. After a nine-year playing career he went into coaching, earning coach of the year honors with Chicago in 2001. (Photograph by Sabby Frinzi.)

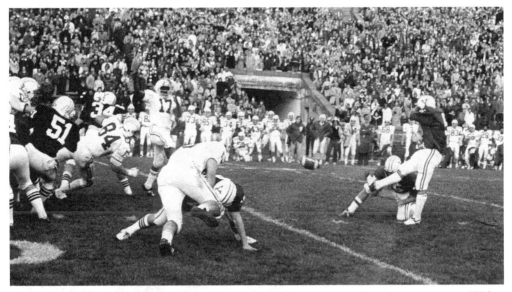

When the Bulldogs hosted Dartmouth in 1975 Carm Cozza needed just one win to tie Walter Camp as the winningest coach in Yale history. Dartmouth went ahead 14-13 with only 44 seconds left, but an overly exuberant celebration drew a 15-yard unsportsmanlike conduct call and Yale got the ball back at its own 44 after the kickoff. A 16-yard completion from Stone Phillips to split end Al Barker helped get the ball to the Dartmouth 30, where Randy Carter nailed a 47-yard field goal to win the game. (Photograph by Sabby Frinzi.)

Stone Phillips emerged as Yale's top quarterback in 1975, throwing for two touchdowns and 165 yards in the season-opening 35-14 win over Connecticut. The following season he led Yale to an Ivy title, earning honorable mention Associated Press All-New England and National Football Hall of Fame Scholar-Athlete honors. A philosophy major, he won Yale's Francis Gordon Brown Award for outstanding academic and athletic leadership. Phillips went on to an Emmy Award-winning career in television. (Photograph by Sabby Frinzi.)

Yale's 100th captain was Vic Staffieri, an offensive lineman. Staffieri led Yale to an 8-1 record and an Ivy League championship in 1976. He was named to the second team on the Ivy League's Silver Anniversary All-Star Football Team in 1981. His 1976 team was to be the last coached by Carm Cozza, who accepted the Yale athletic director job earlier that year with the stipulation that he had to give up his coaching duties at the end of the season. (Photograph by Sabby Frinzi.)

VERY CAPABLE HANDS

8

BACK FOR MORE

"I am first and above all else a football coach," wrote Carm Cozza in a letter to the Yale Corporation in November 1976. As agreed when he became athletic director, Cozza had relinquished his coaching duties at the team banquet the Monday after Yale's win over Harvard. But after five agonizing days he realized where his loyalties lay. With that November letter he informed the corporation that he was giving up the athletic director job to continue coaching. (Photograph by Sabby Frinzi.)

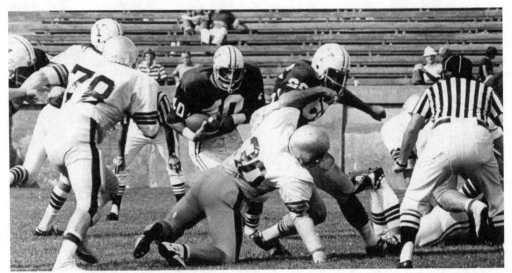

A product of nearby Derby, tailback John Pagliaro (No. 40) was a hometown hero. He broke Dick Jauron's single-season rushing record in 1977, finishing with 1,159 yards and 14 touchdowns as Yale won the Ivy title. That earned him his second straight Ivy League MVP award and All-America status. Among Pagliaro's blockers was guard Steve Carfora (No. 66), who was selected to the second team on the Ivy League's Silver Anniversary All-Star Football Team in 1981 along with Pagliaro. (Photograph by Sabby Frinzi.)

On his way to an 11-year NFL career, John Spagnola (second from left) broke the school career record for passes caught (88) in 1978. Still, his most memorable play was a pass he threw. The tight end devised "Downtown Left" with quarterback Pat O'Brien and tight end Bob Krystyniak (third from left). The Bulldogs executed the play from their 23 yard-line in the second quarter of a 14-14 game against Harvard. Spagnola dropped back to catch a lateral pass from O'Brien, then threw to Krystyniak, who took off for the score en route to a 35-28 Yale win. Here the two celebrate with athletic director Frank Ryan (left) and Yale president A. Bartlett Giamatti (right). (Photograph by Sabby Frinzi.)

BACK FOR MORE

Linebacker Bill Crowley (left) and end Clint Streit (right) make a tackle against UConn in 1978. Crowley led Yale in tackles for three years, meriting All-Ivy honors twice and honorable mention Associated Press All-America selection as a senior. An Academic All-American, member of Phi Beta Kappa, and a National Football Foundation and Hall of Fame Scholar-Athlete, he earned an NCAA postgraduate scholarship and a Rhodes scholarship. Streit was a two-time All-Ivy selection and second team member of the Ivy League's Silver Anniversary All-Star Football Team in 1981. (Photograph by Sabby Frinzi.)

Running back Ken Hill led Yale in rushing in 1978 and 1979, and set an Ivy League record by returning a kickoff 100 yards against Cornell in 1978. The Oakland Raiders converted him to defensive back after selecting him in the 1980 draft, and he went on to spend 10 years in the NFL. (Photograph by Sabby Frinzi.)

Linebacker Tim Tumpane became the first defensive player to earn the Ivy League's Bushnell Cup as MVP with a dominating performance for Yale's 1979 Ivy League championship squad. The team captain, Tumpane finished with 148 tackles and anchored a defense that led the nation in total defense (175.4 yards per game) and rushing defense (75 yards per game). (Photograph by Sabby Frinzi.)

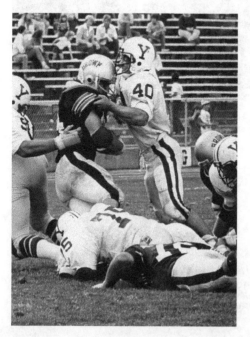

"If you had an instrument that could measure the level of energy a player expends during the course of a football game, Kevin's reading would probably break the instrument." Thus Carm Cozza summed up Kevin Czinger, a five-foot-10-inch middle guard listed generously at 200 pounds who terrorized opposing offenses from 1978 through 1980. Cozza called him the toughest player he coached, typified by his game against Air Force as a senior. Just days after a debilitating stomach virus sent him to the hospital, Czinger made 15 tackles and recovered a pair of fumbles in the 17-16 win. He was named honorable mention All-America and Ivy League MVP. (Photograph by Sabby Frinzi.)

BACK FOR MORE

John Nitti (right, celebrating with trainer Billy Kaminsky) captained the Bulldogs to another Ivy title in 1980. The Bulldogs had clinched a share of the crown by the time they faced Harvard, but needed a victory to earn the title outright. With tailback Rich Diana limited by a neck injury, the Bulldogs pounded away with their fullback Nitti. He finished with 19 carries for 69 yards, including several huge first downs and a touchdown for the 14-0 final. (Photograph by Sabby Frinzi.)

Rich Diana eclipsed Dick Jauron's single-game Yale rushing record twice in 1981. After racking up 196 yards against Brown, he ran for 222 against Princeton—despite two broken fingers and cracked ribs. Shown here scoring in the 28-0 win over Harvard that clinched a share of the Ivy championship, he finished with a school-record 1,442 yards. Named Ivy League MVP, he finished 10th in the Heisman Trophy balloting and earned All-America and Academic All-America honors. Diana had a brief stint in the NFL before turning to a career in medicine. (Photograph by Sabby Frinzi.)

John Rogan (shown here playing in Yale's first night game, 1980 at Boston College) passed up Boston College, Syracuse, and Virginia to come to Yale in 1978, following in the footsteps of his brother Kevin as a Bulldog quarterback. He earned his first start by the second game of his sophomore season, a 24-17 win over UConn, and went on to become the first player to lead Yale in passing for three straight seasons since Dean Loucks did so from 1954 through 1956. (Photograph by Sabby Frinzi.)

After seeing sparse action as a sophomore in 1978, split end Curt Grieve took two semesters off from school. He started out as a draftsman in Los Angeles, but returned home to work at a steel mill in Pittsburgh after gas prices surged. He eventually bought a motorcycle for a ride around the country. Grieve returned to Yale refocused in 1980, grabbing a team-high 32 receptions. His 51 catches in 1981 eclipsed Gary Fencik's school record by nine. (Photograph by Sabby Frinzi.)

BACK FOR MORE

A part of three Ivy League championships, linebacker Jeff Rohrer led the Elis in tackles as a senior in 1981 with 136. Rohrer was Dallas' second-round pick in the 1982 NFL draft. He appeared in 84 games over six seasons in the NFL. (Photograph by Sabby Frinzi.)

The Bulldogs showed what they were capable of in week three of the 1981 season after falling behind heavily favored Navy 12-0. A field goal by Tony Jones and a John Rogan-to-Tom Kokoska touchdown got the Bulldogs within three at halftime. Rogan and Curt Grieve connected for a touchdown in the third to give Yale a 16-12 lead, but Navy went back up on a touchdown early in the fourth. Rogan and Grieve put Yale on top for good, 23-19, with a touchdown with 3:19 to play.

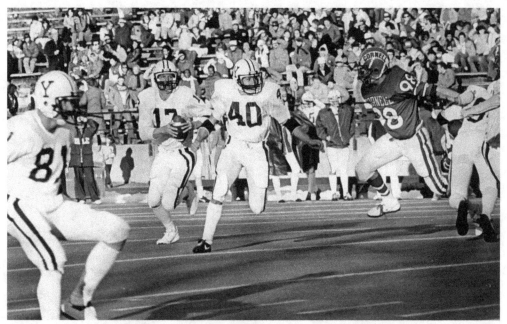

Tailback Paul Andrie (No. 40) had a bone disease and hip problem as a child that put him in braces from the waist down for three years and left doubt as to whether he would ever walk normally. He wound up leading Yale in rushing in 1982 and 1983 (when he played with a broken arm), finishing his career with 2,010 yards. Joe Dufek (No. 17) was Yale's leading passer in 1982 with 1,284 yards and went on to spend two seasons in the NFL. (Photograph by Sabby Frinzi.)

The Game sometimes attracts the attention of pranksters from other schools. During a break in the action in the first quarter of the 1982 edition at Harvard Stadium, a large balloon popped up from the turf near midfield and slowly expanded to reveal the letters M-I-T.

9

AN ERA COMES TO

AN END

The 100th edition of The Game was greeted with the appropriate pomp and circumstance as Harvard came to the Yale Bowl on November 19, 1983. A crowd of 70,600 packed the stands for the ceremonies. All living captains from both schools were invited to be a part of the coin toss. Thirty-two former Bulldog leaders, dating back to 1913 (Henry Ketcham), joined 1983 captain Tom Giella (center). (Photograph by Sabby Frinzi.)

Arkansas native Roosevelt Thompson returned home each summer to work for then-Gov. Bill Clinton. Double-majoring in political science along with history and economics, the offensive lineman also volunteered at a local school and worked at city hall. A member of Phi Beta Kappa, he received a Rhodes scholarship and planned a career in public service. But driving back to New Haven from spring break in 1984, he was killed in an accident. His funeral in Little Rock was attended by 1,500 people, including Clinton and his wife. (Photograph by Sabby Frinzi.)

Middle guard John Zanieski, whose 21 career sacks are third all-time at Yale, was named All-American and won Yale's Blair Award as team MVP in 1984. The Bulldogs went 6-3 that season, including a 27-24 comeback win over Princeton. The Eli defense stopped the Tigers at the two with 1:31 to play and Mike Curtin then completed seven passes in driving 98 yards for the game-winner, a 14-yarder to receiver Kevin Moriarty with five seconds left.

An All-American in track who broke Calvin Hill's school long-jump mark, Eugene Profit started his football career as a receiver. After a move to defensive back his speed attracted the interest of the NFL's New England Patriots in 1986. He went on to spend three years with them and one with the Washington Redskins. After his playing days ended, Profit lived up to his last name by embarking on a career in finance. (Photograph by Sabby Frinzi.)

After graduating in 1985, defensive tackle Jim MacLaren was riding his motorcycle in New York City when a bus crashed into him. Pronounced dead on arrival at Bellevue hospital, MacLaren was resuscitated. He lost his left leg below the knee, but found a new focus: marathons and triathlons. He was competing in one in 1993 when, during the bicycle portion, he was hit by a van. Diagnosed as a quadriplegic, he eventually regained partial use of his limbs. Now a motivational speaker, he earned ESPN's Arthur Ashe Courage Award in 2005. (Photograph by Sabby Frinzi.)

Dean Athanasia came to Yale as a defensive back but soon became an All-Ivy caliber tight end. He led the team in receptions in 1985 and 1986. The following year he surpassed John Spagnola's Yale career record for receptions, ending with 112. (Photograph by Sabby Frinzi.)

Displaying a flair for the comeback, Kelly Ryan quarterbacked his way to the Ivy League MVP award in 1987. Ryan led Yale to fourth-quarter, come-from-behind victories over UConn (threw two touchdown passes in the final two and a half minutes for a 30-27 win); William and Mary (led an 80-yard drive that set up a touchdown with 23 seconds left for a 40-34 win); and Penn (threw the game-winning touchdown pass to Bob Shoop in the final seconds for a 28-22 win). (Photograph by Sabby Frinzi.)

AN ERA COMES TO AN END

After Holy Cross dropped out of a scheduled meeting with Yale in 1987, the Bulldogs found a replacement from afar—very far. A game at Hawaii gave Yale its longest road trip ever. With snow falling back home, the Elis hung with the Rainbows in the 70-degree temperatures until midway through the third quarter, when Hawaii turned a 21-10 game into a 62-10 final. The Bulldogs in this photograph are Kelly Ryan (second from left), athletic director Donald Kagan (fifth from left), Bob Shoop (second from right), and Carm Cozza (right).

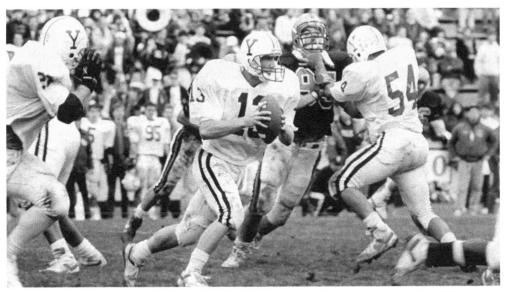

With the top three quarterbacks on his depth chart injured two weeks into the 1988 season, Carm Cozza put in a call to Darin Kehler. Kehler had played freshman football the year before but then opted to concentrate on baseball. With the football team in need, Kehler returned. Just over a month after Cozza's call he took over as the starting quarterback, helping Yale to a win over Dartmouth. He led the Bulldogs to an Ivy championship in 1989, earning first team All-Ivy honors. (Photograph by Sabby Frinzi.)

With three games left in the 1989 season, captain Jon Reese (left, with 1939 captain Bill Stack) was badly injured in a car accident. The linebacker took the field just four days later, wearing a special mouthpiece and face mask because of his broken jaw, and helped Yale to a 34-19 win over Cornell en route to another Ivy League title. (Photograph by Sabby Frinzi.)

Center Mike Ciotti (front left), cornerback Rich Huff (front right), defensive lineman Scott Wollam (back left), defensive lineman Glover Lawrence (back middle), and tight end Jim Griffin (back right) all participated in the 1989 Epson Ivy Bowl in Tokyo, an All-Star game pitting Ivy Leaguers against Japanese players. Huff and Lawrence were first team All-Ivy honorees for Yale's 1989 Ivy championship team. Lawrence's father, Ab, had earned the same honor in 1963. Ciotti's father, Larry, would earn an Ivy championship ring of his own as a Yale assistant coach in 1999.

Captain Chris Kouri ran for 1,101 yards in 1991, earning All-Ivy honors and the Blair Award as team MVP. After graduation Kouri returned home to North Carolina, got his law degree, and ran for Congress in 2002. (Photograph by Sabby Frinzi.)

Tailback Keith Price's 1,141 yards rushing in 1992 place him fifth on Yale's single-season list. A pre-season knee injury the next year forever altered the course of his career. After a grueling rehabilitation process he returned in 1994 and finished his career with 1,809 yards, a figure that places him 10th all-time at Yale. (Photograph by Sabby Frinzi.)

A change in the Ivy League rules for the 1993 season enabled Rob Masella to make history. With freshmen eligible for the varsity again, Masella became the first Ivy freshman since the World War II era to touch a football in varsity play when he returned the opening kickoff against Brown. A defensive back, Masella went on to captain the Bulldogs in 1996.

Six-foot-three-inch, 230-pound Chris Hetherington had not played quarterback before arriving at Yale, but the Bulldogs quickly turned him into a punishing option quarterback. After an injury-plagued start to his career, Hetherington put it all together in 1995. His 1,709 yards of total offense that season rank 10th in school history. To make it as a pro, however, he had to switch positions again. Cincinnati signed him to play fullback, and he eventually made it to the NFL with Indianapolis. (Photograph by Steve Conn.)

Fourteen years after Princeton ended Yale's bid for a perfect season at Palmer Stadium, the Bulldogs returned the favor. The Tigers were 8-0 when the two teams met on November 11, 1995. Yale overcame 7-0 and 13-7 deficits with 14 points in the fourth quarter. Tailback Kena Heffernan's touchdown tied the score at 13 with 3:35 left, and John Stalzer's extra point gave Yale the lead. Later linebacker Matt Siskosky recovered a fumble in the end zone to seal the 21-13 victory. (Photograph by Sabby Frinzi.)

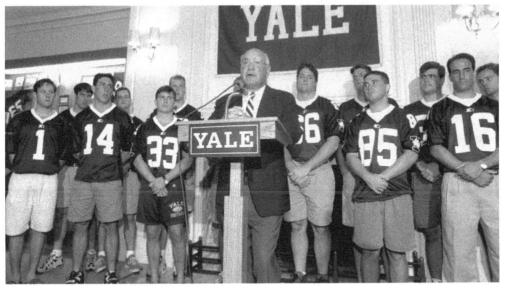

On September 7, 1996, Carm Cozza announced that the upcoming season would be his last as head coach at Yale. Surrounded by his seniors, his family, and a slew of supporters, Cozza explained how difficult his decision was. "It's been a great run," Cozza said. "I've been very fortunate to be part of the family." His 32 seasons included 179 wins and 10 Ivy League titles. He was inducted into the College Football Hall of Fame in 2002. (Photograph by Michael Marsland.)

Jack Siedlecki was named Yale's head coach—an endowed position, the Joel E. Smilow '54 Head Coach of Football—on December 19, 1996. "I have spent my entire career trying to get this job," Siedlecki, who had been at Amherst, said. "I want to be with the best student-athletes because it's fun to coach guys who have that kind of intellect. I have an unbelievable amount of respect for the Yale football tradition." (Photograph by Michael Marsland.)

The Bulldogs' lone win in 1997 came at Soldier Field in Chicago against Valparaiso. The game also marked the emergence of quarterback Joe Walland, who came on in the second quarter to replace an injured Chris Whittaker. Walland led Yale to three touchdowns for the 34-14 win. A part of Carm Cozza's final recruiting class, Walland had switched from defensive back to quarterback and would become a key part of Yale's resurgence. (Photograph by Steve Conn.)

10

RETURN TO GLORY

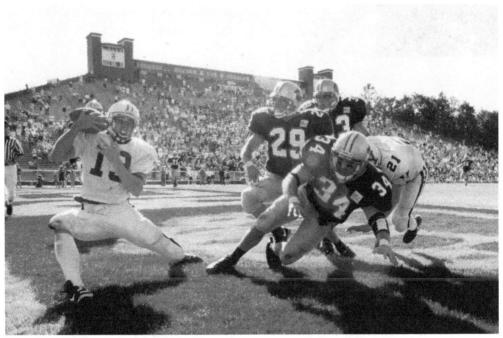

Attempting to erase memories of the 1-9 campaign of 1997, the Bulldogs found themselves trailing 21-10 at Brown in the 1998 opener. A touchdown run by tailback Rashad Bartholomew and a touchdown pass from Joe Walland to tight end Brian Scharf gave Yale a 24-21 lead with 8:52 remaining, but Brown scored the go-ahead touchdown with 59 seconds left. The Bulldogs drove to the Brown 27 for one last play. Walland's heave found receiver Jake Borden in the back of the end zone as time expired for the improbable 30-28 win. (Photograph by Jeff Holt, New Haven Register.)

A transfer from Air Force in 1998, Rashad Bartholomew immediately took over as Yale's starting tailback. With a combination of size (six feet, 215 pounds) and speed, he broke Dick Jauron's Yale career rushing record, finishing with 3,015 yards. Yale went 22-8 in his three seasons. (Photograph by Stephen Fritzer.)

When Yale football broadcasts returned to the airwaves of WELI 960 AM in 1998, the Bulldogs brought back two familiar voices. Dick Galiette (right), who had called Yale games during the glory years from the 1960s through the 1980s, returned as the play-by-play voice of Yale football. Carm Cozza (left) joined him as color commentator. (Photograph by Sabby Frinzi.)

A share of the Ivy title was on the line as Yale trailed Harvard 21-17 with 2:53 to play in the 1999 edition of The Game in front of 52,484 fans at the Yale Bowl. Starting at the Bulldog 42, quarterback Joe Walland began one last comeback. Walland was in the hospital the day before with badly swollen tonsils and a temperature that surpassed 103, spending most of the day hooked up to IVs. He also had a sprained thumb on his left (throwing) hand. Three completions and two scrambles by Walland got the ball to the Harvard 10 with just over a minute to play, and Walland completed a pass to receiver Eric Johnson at the four to set up the decisive play. Johnson beat his man in the end zone, but Walland's pass was deflected at the line of scrimmage and began tumbling to the ground. Johnson stopped, leaned forward, and grabbed the ball just before it hit the ground, winning the game and the Ivy Championship for Yale with 29 seconds left. "The Catch" was Johnson's 21st reception of the game, breaking the previous Ivy League record by six. (Photograph by Sabby Frinzi.)

The Bulldogs led the Ivy League in scoring defense in 1999, allowing only 16 points per game. Stalwarts such as lineman Peter Maloney (left), middle guard Andy Tuzzolino (second from left), linebacker Peter Mazza (third from left), defensive end Jeff Hockenbrock (fourth from left), and defensive end Peter Sarantos (right) led the way. Yale finished the season 9-1, winning its first Ivy League title in 10 years. (Photograph by Steve Conn.)

There was one piece of unfinished business after the 1999 season—the Bulldogs were stuck on 799 wins at the end. They took care of that in the 2000 opener, beating Dayton 42-6 to become the first college team ever to 800. The game ball was sent to the College Football Hall of Fame. (Courtesy Yale Sports Publicity Department.)

RETURN TO GLORY

Gifted with great hands and athleticism, receiver Eric Johnson made countless drive-saving grabs. To make it in the NFL, Johnson bulked up and became a tight end. When he and defensive back Than Merrill were drafted in 2001, it marked the first time any Yale players had been picked since three (Rich Diana, Curt Grieve, and Jeff Rohrer) were chosen in 1982. Johnson led the San Francisco 49ers in receptions with 82 in 2004. (Photograph by Steve Conn.)

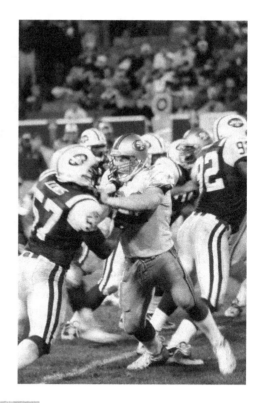

Yale was preparing for its 2001 season opener at Towson when news of the September 11 terrorist attacks hit. The game with the Tigers was cancelled, and the Bulldogs soon learned that they had lost one of their own in the World Trade Center. Defensive tackle Rich Lee, a 1991 graduate, was working for Cantor Fitzgerald when the attacks occurred. (Photograph by Sabby Frinzi.)

Within a span of two years, the class of 2002 was struck by two tragic deaths. Fullback Jim Keppel (right) passed away in 2003 due to a previously undetected heart condition, and defensive back Ryan LoProto (left) perished in Spain in the summer of 2005. Each man was honored by the naming of an award for the top player at his position—offensive back for Keppel, defensive back for LoProto. The first winner of the Keppel Award was tight end Nate Lawrie, who went on to play in the NFL. The inaugural Lo Proto Award went to cornerback Mike Holben. (Photograph by Mike LoProto.)

Receiver Ralph Plumb broke Eric Johnson's career receptions record, registering 79 in 2004 to finish with 195. Plumb, a Rhode Island native, had the game-winning 20-yard reception with 1:46 left in Yale's 31-27 win at Brown in 2002. (Photograph by Ron Waite/Photosportacular; courtesy of Yale Sports Publicity Department.)

Tailback Robert Carr showed signs of greatness in 2001, becoming just the second Bulldog freshman since 1946 to score a touchdown. In the second game of 2002, he ran for a school-record 235 yards in a 50-23 win over Cornell. The following year he led the team in rushing for the second straight season. Prior to the 2004 season, Carr nearly drowned while swimming in a lake. Rescued by a stranger, he went on to finish with a school-record 3,393 career yards. (Photograph by Bill O'Brien.)

Quarterback Alvin Cowan's running and passing accounted for a school-record six touchdowns (three running, three passing) in the first game of the 2002 season, a 49-14 win over San Diego. He suffered a season-ending broken leg in the next game. A year later, Cowan returned and resumed his record-setting ways. He is Yale's career leader (6,024 yards) and single-season leader (3,429 yards, 2003) in total offense. (Photograph by Ron Waite/Photosportacular; courtesy of Yale Sports Publicity Department.)

Coming from western Pennsylvania, Jeff Mroz had the tradition of quarterbacks from that area—including Joe Montana and Joe Namath—ingrained in him early on. He got the chance to start as a sophomore in 2002 after Alvin Cowan was injured, and responded by throwing for 1,731 yards. After Cowan graduated, Mroz again assumed the starting role in 2005, throwing for 2,484 yards and 22 touchdowns. He signed with the Dallas Cowboys as a free agent after the 2006 NFL draft. (Photograph by Ron Waite/Photosportacular; courtesy of Yale Sports Publicity Department.)

The Bulldogs' in-state recruiting efforts paid off when the 2004 Connecticut State Player of the Year, Mike McLeod of New Britain, committed to Yale. McLeod ran for 689 yards as a freshman in 2005, earning Ivy League Rookie of the Year honors. (Photograph by Ron Waite/Photosportacular; courtesy of Yale Sports Publicity Department.)

RETURN TO GLORY

A major gift from Charles Johnson '54, matched by his classmates, enabled Yale to move forward dramatically in its quest to renovate the Yale Bowl in 2004. To honor the contribution, the field was named the Class of 1954 Field. The school also received gifts for the Kenney Family Field Center, a renovated field center with space to be added on top for special functions, and the Jensen Family Plaza, a facility that will lead up to the main entrance and include a listing of each Yale football team since 1872. The Kenney Family Field Center is named in honor of the family that produced five Yale football players (Brian '60, Jerry '63, Robert '67, Richard '71, and Jeff '93), while the Jensen Family Plaza is named after former Bulldogs Irving '54, Colin '57, Erik '63, and Mark '67. By the spring of 2005 construction crews had begun work to restore the inner and outer walls, returning the facility to the condition it was in for its grand opening in 1914. (Photograph by Sam Rubin.)

Visit us at
arcadiapublishing.com